1st EDITION

Perspectives on Modern World History

Chernobyl

1st EDITION

Perspectives on Modern World History
Chernobyl

David Erik Nelson

Book Editor

GREENHAVEN PRESS
A part of Gale, Cengage Learning

GALE
CENGAGE Learning™

Detroit • New York • San Francisco • New Haven, Conn • Waterville, Maine • London

Christine Nasso, *Publisher*
Elizabeth Des Chenes, *Managing Editor*

© 2010 Thomson Gale, a part of Gale, Cengage Learning.

For more information, contact:
Greenhaven Press
27500 Drake Rd.
Farmington Hills, MI 48331-3535
Or you can visit our Internet site at gale.cengage.com

For product information and technology assistance, contact us at
Gale Customer Support, 1-800-877-4253.

For permission to use material from this text or product, submit all requests online at
www.cengage.com/permissions.

Further permissions questions can be emailed to permissionrequest@cengage.com

LIBRARY OF CONGRESS CATALOGING-IN-PUBLICATION DATA

Chernobyl / David Erik Nelson, book editor.
    p. cm. -- (Perspectives on modern world history)
    Includes bibliographical references and index.
ISBN 978-0-7377-4555-9 (hardcover)
1. Chernobyl Nuclear Accident, Chornobyl?, Ukraine, 1986--History. 2. Nuclear power plants--Accidents--Ukraine--Chornobyl?. I. Nelson, David Erik.
    TK1362.U38C42 2009
    363.17'99094777--dc22
                                                        2009027203

Printed in the United States of America
2 3 4 5 6 7 13 12 11 10

CONTENTS

David R. Marples

On April 26, 1986, a poorly planned safety test
resulted in the explosion of the reactor in unit
four of the Chernobyl Nuclear Power Plant in
Ukraine. The subsequent release of radioactive material forced the evacuation of 135,000
people—including Pripyat's entire population
of 45,000—and badly contaminated roughly
100,000 square miles of land in the agricultural heart of Eastern Europe.

David F. Duke

The author describes the development of both
the military and civil nuclear industries in the
Soviet Union, including technical aspects of
the Soviet-style RBMK reactor, whose design
shortcomings were directly responsible for the
Chernobyl catastrophe.

physicist and expert in nuclear technology deems that the recovery efforts were not simply sufficient, but even commendable.

CHAPTER 3   Personal Narratives

cized in their new communities and ignored
by their government.

FOREWORD

*"History cannot give us a program for the future,
but it can give us a fuller understanding of ourselves, and of our common humanity, so that we
can better face the future."*

—*Robert Penn Warren,
American poet and novelist*

The history of each nation is punctuated by momen-
tous events that represent turning points for that
nation, with an impact felt far beyond its borders.
These events—displaying the full range of human capa-
bilities, from violence, greed, and ignorance to heroism,
courage, and strength—are nearly always complicated
and multifaceted. Any student of history faces the chal-
lenge of grasping the many strands that constitute such
world-changing events as wars, social movements, and
environmental disasters. But understanding these significant historic events can be enhanced by exposure
to a variety of perspectives, whether of people involved
intimately or of ones observing from a distance of miles
or years. Understanding can also be increased by learning about the controversies surrounding such events and
exploring hot-button issues from multiple angles. Finally,
true understanding of important historic events involves
knowledge of the events' human impact—of the ways
such events affected people in their everyday lives—all
over the world.

Perspectives on Modern World History examines
global historic events from the twentieth-century onward
by presenting analysis and observation from numerous
vantage points. Each volume offers high school, early
college level, and general interest readers a thematically

arranged anthology of previously published materials that address a major historical event, with an emphasis on international coverage. Each volume opens with background information on the event, then presents the controversies surrounding that event, and concludes with first-person narratives from people who lived through the event or were affected by it. By providing primary sources from the time of the event, as well as relevant commentary surrounding the event, this series can be used to inform debate, help develop critical thinking skills, increase global awareness, and enhance an understanding of international perspectives on history.

Material in each volume is selected from a diverse range of sources, including journals, magazines, newspapers, nonfiction books, personal narratives, speeches, congressional testimony, government documents, pamphlets, organization newsletters, and position papers. Articles taken from these sources are carefully edited and introduced to provide context and background. Each volume of Perspectives on Modern World History includes an array of views on events of global significance. Much of the material comes from international sources and from U.S. sources that provide extensive international coverage.

Each volume in the Perspectives on Modern World History series also includes:

- A full-color **world map**, offering context and geographic perspective.
- An annotated **table of contents** that provides a brief summary of each essay in the volume.
- An **introduction** specific to the volume topic.
- For each viewpoint, a brief **introduction** that has notes about the author and source of the viewpoint, and that provides a summary of its main points.
- Full-color **charts**, **graphs**, **maps**, and other visual representations.

- Informational **sidebars** that explore the lives of key individuals, give background on historical events, or explain scientific or technical concepts.
- A **glossary** that defines key terms, as needed.
- A **chronology** of important dates preceding, during, and immediately following the event.
- A **bibliography** of additional books, periodicals, and Web sites for further research.
- A comprehensive **subject index** that offers access to people, places, and events cited in the text.

Perspectives on Modern World History is designed for a broad spectrum of readers who want to learn more about not only history but also current events, political science, government, international relations, and sociology—students doing research for class assignments or debates, teachers and faculty seeking to supplement course materials, and others wanting to improve their understanding of history. Each volume of Perspectives on Modern World History is designed to illuminate a complicated event, to spark debate, and to show the human perspective behind the world's most significant happenings of recent decades.

INTRODUCTION

On April 26, 1986, at 1:23:44 A.M., a massive steam explosion tore apart reactor four of the V.I. Lenin Nuclear Power Station near the city of Chernobyl, in what was then the breadbasket of the Soviet Union. Forty seconds earlier, engineers at the plant had begun powering down the reactor for an ill-conceived safety experiment that had been proposed the previous morning. Owing to the design of the reactor, a constant flow of water was needed to cool the reactor core—even when the reactor was "turned off." Although it was a vital part of the reactor's design, engineers had never actually confirmed that reactor four could continue normal cooling operations during a power outage. The facility's day shift was fully briefed on the experiment, and at 2 P.M. some emergency core cooling systems were taken offline and the plant began to wind down. When a regional power station unexpectedly went offline, reactor four was brought back to full power and the test delayed past the evening peak-demand period.

Preparations for the experiment resumed at 11:04 P.M., long after the day shift had left, and as the evening shift was preparing to clock out. The night shift was due at midnight. Some of the original day-shift electrical engineers—who had by then been working for upwards of fifteen hours—stayed on, but the night shift was largely unprepared to run the experiment. A less-experienced night shift control-rod operator, Leonid Toptunov, inadvertently inserted the control rods too far, nearly shutting down the reactor. At 12:32 A.M., in an apparent attempt to compensate for the error, he overrode automatic safety controls and pulled the rods back beyond their safety margin. This restored some power, but was still lower than the minimum prescribed for the experiment. In order to prevent the reactor from automatically shutting down under these conditions, the operator deactivated both the remaining emergency core cooling system and several "SCRAM" (emergency shutdown) circuits at 1:15 A.M.

At 1:19 A.M. extra water pumps were activated, as part of the experiment, decreasing the reactor's power output. To compensate, Toptunov pulled the control rods farther out of the core. At 1:23 A.M. the reactor crew began the experiment by disconnecting a power-supply turbine, simulating a power outage. Owing to several unforeseen factors, powering the reactor down in this manner caused it, counterintuitively, to temporarily heat up and produce more power. After forty seconds Toptunov, evidently concerned about the mounting heat, initiated a rapid emergency shutdown of the reactor, or "SCRAM," in which all control rods are fully reinserted. Because of a flaw in the design of the tips of the graphite control rods, the rapid shutdown—which actually took up to twenty seconds—displaced water coolant, causing a serious power spike. Increasing heat within the reactor caused the rods to swell and jam their channels before they could be fully inserted and halt the reaction. The reactor surged. The graphite control rods melted, and rapidly increasing steam pressure blasted the two-thousand-ton biological protection shield from the reactor's top, exposing the reactor core to the open air. Oxygen poured in and ignited the graphite. The super-heated graphite then seeped into the emergency cooling pool beneath the reactor, steam billowed up, and a second, more powerful steam explosion threw uranium and burning graphite onto surrounding buildings, including reactor three (which was still operating normally), causing multiple fires. Two engineers were killed in the blasts. Despite receiving the heaviest dose of initial radiation, the control-rod operator, Toptunov, stayed at the reactor for hours, frantically working in the rescue efforts. He was dead of acute radiation poisoning within two weeks, the same day that the fire was finally extinguished in reactor four's core.

The first crew of fourteen firefighters arrived at 1:28 A.M.—five minutes after the experiment had begun—and within a half-hour were joined by another hundred from the nearby town of Pripyat. Meanwhile, the exposed reactor and uranium released an unknown amount of radiation and radioactive steam. At 8:00 A.M., less than seven hours after the accident, the reactor's day shift clocked in, as usual, and a 286-man crew continued construction on nearby reactors five and six.

Despite the precision of the timing details—the experiment resuming at 11:04 P.M., Toptunov hitting the SCRAM button at 1:23:40 A.M., there being an explosion at 1:23:44 A.M., 286 construction workers arriving at 8:00 A.M., et cetera—Chernobyl is emblematic of the terror of not knowing: There is no consensus on the lasting impact of the accident; whether the "Zone of Alienation," (the most contaminated area, a nineteen-mile radius of reactor four) is still toxic or perfectly safe; whether children should drink Belorusian milk; or whether tourists should tromp around the eerie, abandoned town of Pripyat. It cannot even be said with confidence how much of the radioactive core is sealed within the crumbling concrete sarcophagus now covering the remains of reactor four: The amount of radiation spewing from the breached core (currently estimated at twenty thousand roentgen per hour—two hundred times the lethal dose) was higher than the only functional radiation detectors accessible on site could measure. No one knows how much of the core drifted away as smoke during the course of the two-week long graphite fire, ultimately falling on Russia, Belarus, Ukraine, Moldova, Turkey, the Black Sea, Macedonia, Serbia, Croatia, Bosnia-Herzegovina, Bulgaria, Greece, Romania, Lithuania, Estonia, Latvia, Finland, Denmark,

Norway, Sweden, Austria, Hungary, the Czech Republic, the Slovak Republic, the Netherlands, Belgium, Slovenia, Poland, Switzerland, Germany, Luxembourg, Italy, Ireland, France, the United Kingdom, and the Atlantic Ocean.

According to the International Atomic Energy Agency's Chernobyl Forum, there were a total of six hundred thousand registered "liquidators"—workers and soldiers who helped in immediate rescue efforts and long-term cleanup at the site—of whom fewer than half absorbed significant doses of radiation (equal to having a thousand chest X-rays over the course of a few months). But these registries of liquidators didn't exist until 1989, three years after the accident. Other reports estimate that up to 1 million men were pressed into service as liquidators, that 20 percent of them died as a result, and 80 percent experience lingering, often inexplicable, health issues. There are many reliable accounts of Soviet doctors refusing to attribute illnesses to radioactive fallout from the Chernobyl accident, and death certificates reading "pneumonia" and even "sore throat," rather than "radiation sickness." State-run orphanages in Belarus—a tiny nation whose land absorbed the brunt of the atomic fallout from the Chernobyl disaster— are crowded with children, called "Chernobyl orphans," exhibiting both perfectly diagnosable cancers and occasionally bizarre developmental delays and birth defects.

Meanwhile, the Chernobyl Forum reports with complete confidence that the official death toll for the Chernobyl accident is fifty-six: twenty-eight firemen, plant workers, and other "liquidators" died in 1986 as an immediate consequence of the accident; between 1987 and 2004, nineteen more workers succumbed to cancers attributable to the radioactivity. In that same period, nine children died of thyroid cancer, the result of absorbing radioactive iodine-131 released during the explosion and fire.

But even though elevated levels of radioactive strontium-90 and cesium-137 can still be easily detected throughout the Zone of Alienation, this area has blossomed into a pristine environmental preserve. In her book *Wormwood Forest: A Natural History of Chernobyl*, Mary Mycio notes that the region, despite increased levels of radiation, is home to thriving populations of deer, lynx, beavers, and even rare black storks. In *Flat Earth News: An Award-Winning Reporter Exposes Falsehood, Distortion and Propaganda in the Global Media*, British journalist Nick Davies likewise cites research showing that generations of mice and voles who have freely scampered around the decommissioned nuclear power facility for decades show no signs of ill-health. All of these animals are doing fine, despite eating, sleeping, and breeding in the shadow of history's worst industrial catastrophe.

The contributors to *Perspectives on Modern World History: Chernobyl* offer many fascinating, and often contradictory, views of this disaster and its lasting impact. They explore these over the course of three chapters, titled "Historical Background on the Chernobyl Disaster," "Controversies Surrounding the Chernobyl Disaster," and "Personal Narratives," the latter composed of accounts of those who survived the disaster or witnessed its aftermath.

World Map

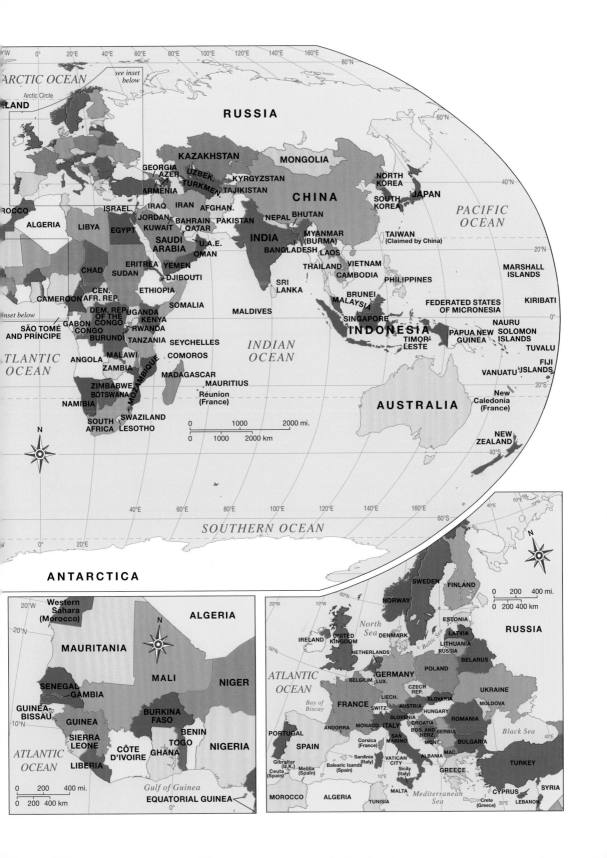

CHAPTER 1

Historical Background on the Chernobyl Disaster

The Chernobyl Disaster

David R. Marples

David R. Marples is a professor at the University of Alberta, Canada, where he specializes in Russian and Ukrainian history. His 1986 book, *Chernobyl and Nuclear Power in the USSR*, is the earliest detailed account of both the Soviet nuclear power industry and the Chernobyl accident itself. In the following viewpoint, Marples gives an overview of the events leading up to the April 26, 1986, explosion of reactor 4 at the V.I. Lenin Nuclear Power Station near Chernobyl, Ukraine. He explains both the immediate health impact of the explosion, as well as the long-term effects the radioactive contamination has had on the population of Ukraine and Belarus and the ongoing dangers posed by the crumbling containment shroud around the remains of the reactor and its exposed core.

T he disaster at Chernobyl (Ukrainian spelling: Chornobyl) on April 26, 1986 occurred as a result of an experiment on how long safety equipment would function during shutdown at the fourth reactor unit at Ukraine's first and largest nuclear power station.

Photo on previous page: The Chernobyl power plant, just after the world's worst nuclear accident on April 6, 1986. (**AP Images.**)

SOURCE. David R. Marples, *Encyclopedia of Russian History*. Belmont, CA: Macmillan Reference USA, 2004. Copyright © 2004 Thomson Gale. Reproduced by permission of Gale, a part of Cengage Learning.

The operators had dismantled safety mechanisms at the reactor to prevent its automatic shutdown, but this reactor type (a graphite moderated Soviet RBMK) became unstable if operated at low power. An operator error caused a power surge that blew the roof off the reactor unit, releasing the contents of the reactor into the atmosphere for a period of about twelve days.

The accident contaminated an area of about 100,000 square miles. This area encompassed about 20 percent of the territory of Belarus; about 8 percent of Ukraine; and about 0.5–1.0 percent of the Russian Federation. Altogether the area is approximately the size of the state of Kentucky or of Scotland and Northern Ireland combined. The most serious radioactive elements to be disseminated by the accident were Iodine-131, Cesium-137, and Strontium-90. The authorities contained the graphite fire with sand and boron, and coal miners constructed a shelf underneath it to prevent it from falling into the water table.

> According to statistics from the Ukrainian government, more than 12,000 'liquidators' died, the majority of which were young men between the ages of twenty and forty.

Evacuations

After the accident, about 135,000 people were evacuated from settlements around the reactor, including the town of Pripyat (population 45,000), the home of the plant workers and their families, and the town of Chernobyl (population 10,000), though the latter remained the center of the cleanup operations for several years. The initial evacuation zone was a 30-kilometer (about 18.6 miles) radius around the destroyed reactor unit. After the spring of 1989 the authorities published maps to show that radioactive fallout had been much more extensive, and approximately 250,000 people subsequently moved to new homes.

Though the Soviet authorities did not release accurate information about the accident, and classified the health data, under international pressure they sent a team of experts to a meeting of the IAEA (The International Atomic Energy Agency) in August 1986, which revealed some of the causes of the accident. The IAEA in turn was allowed to play a key role in improving the safety of Soviet RBMK reactors, though it did not demand the closure of the plant until 1994. A trial of Chernobyl managers took place in 1987, and the plant director and chief engineer received sentences of hard labor, ten and five years respectively.

The "company town" of Pripyat, Ukraine, has been deserted since the catastrophe at the Chernobyl Nuclear Power Plant in Ukraine (background). (Yuri Kozyrev/ Newsmakers/Getty Images.)

Long-Term Effects of the Accident

Chernobyl remains shrouded in controversy as to its immediate and long-term effects. The initial explosion and graphite fire killed thirty-one operators, firemen,

What Is Radiation?

The word *radiation* comes from a Latin term that means "ray of light." It is used in a general sense to cover all forms of energy that travel through space in the form of "rays." Radiation may occur in the form of a stream of subatomic particles, like miniature bullets from a machine gun, or in the form of electromagnetic waves. Subatomic particles are the basic units of matter and energy (electrons, neutrons, protons, neutrinos, and positrons), which are even smaller than atoms. Electromagnetic waves are a form of energy that includes light itself, as well as other forms of energy such as X rays, gamma rays, radio waves, and radar.

In addition, the word *radiation* is sometimes used to describe the transfer of heat from a hot object to a cooler one that is not touching the first object. . . .

When some people hear the word *radiation*, they think of the radiation that comes from radioactive materials. This radiation consists of both particles and electromagnetic waves. Both forms of radiation can be harmful because they carry a great deal of energy. When they come into contact with atoms, they tend to tear the atoms apart by removing electrons from them. This damage to atoms may cause materials

and first-aid workers and saw several thousand hospitalized. Over the summer of 1986 up until 1990, it also caused high casualties among cleanup workers ["liquidators"]. According to statistics from the Ukrainian government, more than 12,000 "liquidators" died, the majority of which were young men between the ages of twenty and forty. A figure of 125,000 deaths issued by the Ukrainian ministry of health in 1996 appears to include all subsequent deaths, natural or otherwise, of those living in the contaminated zone of Ukraine.

According to specialists from the WHO (World Health Organization) the most discernible health impact of the high levels of radiation in the affected territories has been the dramatic rise in thyroid gland cancer among children. In Belarus, for example, a 1994 study noted that to undergo changes that can be harmful or damaging. For example, plastics exposed to radiation from radioactive sources can become very brittle. . . .

High-energy radiation, such as that of X rays and gamma rays, is also called ionizing radiation, a name that comes from the ability of the radiation to remove electrons from atoms. The particles left behind when electrons are removed are called ions. Ionizing radiation can cause serious damage to both living and nonliving materials. . . .

Large doses of any kind of radiation, ionizing or not, can be dangerous. Too much sunlight, for example, can damage a person's eyes or skin. Lasers can deliver such intense beams of light that they can burn through metal—not to mention human flesh. The energy from microwaves in ovens is high enough to cook meats and vegetables.

On the other hand, small amounts of any kind of radiation are generally thought to be harmless. Even low doses of ionizing radiation from radioactive materials is probably not dangerous. The latter fact is of special importance because radioactive materials occur in small concentrations all around us.

SOURCE. *"Radiation,"* UXL Encyclopedia of Science, *Rob Nagel, ed., 2nd ed. Detroit: UXL, 2007.*

congenital defects in the areas with a cesium content of the soil of one–five curies [a unit of radioactivity] per square kilometer have doubled since 1986, while in areas with more than fifteen curies, the rise has been more than eight times the norm.

Among liquidators and especially among evacuees, studies have demonstrated a discernible and alarming rise in morbidity [the relative incidence of disease] since Chernobyl when compared to the general population. This applies particularly to circulatory and digestive diseases, and to respiratory problems. Less certain is the concept referred to as "Chernobyl AIDS," the rise of which may reflect more attention to medical problems, better access to health care, or psychological fears and tension among the population living in contaminated

> The correlation between thyroid gland cancer and radioactive fallout appears clear and is not negated by any medical authorities.

zones. Rises in children's diabetes and anemia are evident, and again appear much higher in irradiated zones. The connection between these problems and the rise in radiation content of the soil have yet to be determined.

Increasing Cancer Rates

To date, the rates of leukemia and lymphoma—though they have risen since the accident—remain within the European average, though in the upper seventy-fifth percentile. One difficulty here is the unreliability or sheer lack of reporting in the 1970s. The induction period for leukemia is four to fifteen years, thus it appears premature to state, as some authorities have, that Chernobyl will not result in higher rates of leukemia.

As for thyroid cancer, its development has been sudden and rapid. As of 2003 about 2,000 children in Belarus and Ukraine have contracted the disease and it is expected to reach its peak in 2005. One WHO specialist has estimated that the illness may affect one child in ten living in the irradiated zones in the summer of 1986; hence ultimate totals could reach as high as 10,000. Though the mortality rate from this form of cancer among children is only about 10 percent, this still indicates an additional 1,000 deaths in the future. Moreover, this form of cancer is highly aggressive and can spread rapidly if not operated on. The correlation between thyroid gland cancer and radioactive fallout appears clear and is not negated by any medical authorities.

After pressure from the countries of the G7 [Canada, France, Germany, Italy, Japan, UK, and USA], Ukraine first imposed a moratorium on any new nuclear reactors (lifted in 1995) and then closed down the Chernobyl station at the end of the year 2000. The key issue at Chernobyl remains the construction and funding of a

new roof over the destroyed reactor, the so-called sarcophagus. The current structure, which contains some
twenty tons of radioactive fuel and dust, is cracking and
is not expected to last more than ten years. There are fears
of the release of radioactive dust within the confines of
the station and beyond should the structure collapse.

A Lingering Hazard

It is fair to say that the dangers presented by former
Soviet nuclear power stations in 2003 exceed those of a
decade earlier. In the meantime, some 3.5 million people
continue to live in contaminated zones. From a necessary
panacea, evacuation of those living in zones with high
soil contamination today has become an unpopular and
slow-moving process. Elderly people in particular have
returned to their homes in some areas.

The Development of the Soviet Nuclear Industry

David F. Duke

In the following viewpoint David F. Duke traces the development of the Soviet nuclear energy program. He argues that the program, rooted in the paranoid secrecy of the Cold War nuclear arms race, focused on productivity at the expense of stability and safety. This resulted in a large number of ill-designed reactors and processing facilities being brought online over a very short period of time. Predictably, there were many severe accidents that went unreported and insufficiently remedied. Duke goes on to point out how, following the disintegration of the Soviet Union in 1991, many former Soviet satellites and republics were dependent on nuclear power, despite their inability to maintain their facilities or process the nuclear waste. Although the Chernobyl accident became a symbol of the failures of the Communist system, the Eastern European nuclear industry itself has recovered, and even flourished, since the collapse of the Soviet Union.

Joseph Stalin, the leader of the Soviet Union during World War II (in Soviet history properly called the Great Patriotic War, from 1941–1945), was well aware that the United States was considering the construction of a new kind of weapon—the atomic bomb—even before the initiation of the Manhattan Project in the United States in late 1942. Information had been supplied to the Soviet Union by a German-born but British-naturalized scientist, Klaus Fuchs. Fuchs had been reporting on Britain's experiments in the field in 1941 and 1942. When he joined the Manhattan Project in November 1943 he continued to pass information of high quality to his Soviet contacts. Initially, however, Stalin did not appreciate the significance of the atomic bomb, and he directed that only a small research endeavor should be undertaken.

At most two dozen Soviet scientists, led by physicist Igor Kurchatov (1903–1960), worked on the project prior to 1944, and they focused their efforts primarily on the theoretical challenges of nuclear fission. In any case, in 1942 and 1943 the Soviet Union was still hard-pressed in its war with Nazi Germany, and more immediate production priorities, such as tanks and aircraft, occupied center stage. The equipment required by an atomic research program was simply unavailable to Kurchatov and his team.

The reports supplied by Fuchs after his move to Los Alamos, New Mexico (the headquarters of the Manhattan Project), along with the Trinity atomic test at Alamogordo, New Mexico, in July 1945, and the destruction of Hiroshima and Nagasaki, Japan, by atomic bombs the following month, all convinced Stalin that the Soviet Union could not afford to fall too far behind the American effort. The Soviet atomic bomb program was

> The scientist Mikhail Klochko suggested that as many as 50,000 to 100,000 lives were lost . . . in the first decade [of Soviet nuclear development] alone.

therefore reorganized, accelerated and, most of all, dramatically expanded in late 1945.

Rapid Nuclear Development

In January 1946 at a meeting with Kurchatov, Stalin is reported (in notes found in the Archive of the Kurchatov Institute in Moscow) to have said it was "not worth spending time and effort on small-scale work." Instead the Soviet scientific and engineering establishment would have to "conduct the work broadly, on a Russian scale, and that in this regard the broadest, utmost assistance" would be provided, especially an "investment of a decisive quantity of resources." It was a statement that signaled a shift of political emphasis: beginning in 1946 the construction of an atomic bomb would be the highest priority of the Soviet Union's political leadership, higher even than reconstruction of the damage inflicted by four years of terrible war with Germany.

> Two of the fundamental characteristics of the Soviet atomic effort [were] its secretiveness . . . and its willingness to pursue whatever means were necessary.

Stalin got his bomb, and he got it quickly. In August 1949, only four years after the Manhattan Project had borne fruit in the deserts of New Mexico, the Soviet Union detonated its first atomic device. Characteristically, the news was kept a secret. It was high-altitude sampling by American aircraft over the Pacific Ocean that detected the unambiguous radioactive evidence of a Soviet nuclear test. The U.S. political and military establishment was shocked; all but the most hawkish of projections had bluntly stated that the Soviet Union would take until the mid-1950s to construct nuclear weapons. The Soviets had beaten those projections by more than five years.

The cost of that rapid development to the Soviet people and the Soviet environment, however, was enormous. It is significant that the man in charge of directing the overall atomic program was Stalin's secret police chief, Lavrentii Beria. Beria's other responsibilities included running the notorious Soviet concentration camp system, or *gulag*, where political prisoners and other "enemies of the state" were sentenced to long terms of hard labor in unspeakable conditions. Tasked with producing uranium for the atomic bomb program, Beria simply used concentration camp labor to mine and process the radioactive material.

No Safety Precautions

No safety precautions, such as dust masks or protective clothing, were undertaken to shield the prisoners against the dangers of radioactivity. This use of slave labor was extraordinarily profligate in terms of human losses. The scientist Mikhail Klochko suggested that as many as 50,000 to 100,000 lives were lost in the process in the first decade alone, and other authorities concur that casualties were probably in the tens of thousands.

In addition to the mining and semi-processing effort, a series of processing and manufacturing complexes were constructed, almost all of them in the interior of Russia east of the Ural Mountains. These centers, known only by postal code numbers and a name associated with nearby settlements, quickly grew into small cities closed to the outside world. In the late 1940s and 1950s at places like Chelyabinsk-65, Krasnoyarsk-26, and Tomsk-7, a massive research and productive effort grew up involving tens of thousands of engineers, scientists, and common workers.

Unlike the slave labor suffering in the mines, the scientists and engineers lived a cosseted existence by Soviet standards, supplied with the best consumer goods available, provided with lavish housing allowances (again, by Soviet standards), and given generous holiday benefits. Common workers at these sites, however, suffered a far more difficult existence, exposed on a regular basis

> "Chelyabinsk-65 was . . . the site of the largest accident in nuclear history prior to the 1986 accident at Chernobyl."

to radioactive hazards that in many cases proved fatal.

Thus, very early in the program are seen two of the fundamental characteristics of the Soviet atomic effort: its secretiveness remarkable even in comparison to the top-secret nuclear programs of the United States and, later, those of the United Kingdom and France and its willingness to pursue whatever means were necessary to produce the required arsenal. Both of these characteristics would profoundly affect the Soviet experience with nuclear weapons, nuclear power, and the waste produced by both programs.

Expansion and Problems of the Program

When Stalin died in March 1953 the Soviet atomic weapons effort was well advanced. The knowledge and technical expertise derived from the test of August 1949 and its aftermath allowed the burgeoning weapons infrastructure to develop techniques of repetitive and later mass production of weapons-grade plutonium and uranium. In 1953 the Red Army received its first shipment of deployable atomic weapons, and in August of that year the Soviet Union surprised the world once again, this time with its test of a thermonuclear (or "hydrogen") bomb, a weapon hundreds or thousands of times more powerful than those dropped on Hiroshima and Nagasaki. In doing so it demonstrated that the gap with the United States had closed dramatically—the latter had tested its first thermonuclear device not years but only months earlier, in November 1952.

The expanding nuclear weapons infrastructure that supported these remarkable advances was by no means trouble-free, however. Indeed, since the collapse of the Soviet Union in 1991 the true scale of the nuclear accidents, environmental contamination, and public health impact of the nuclear weapons program has become clear. At Chelyabinsk-65 (now called the Mayak Production Association) alone there were dozens, perhaps hundreds, of accidents in the 1940s and 1950s that claimed the lives of many plant workers.

Many of these accidents were caused by the feverish pitch of the work, which emphasized speed over safety and productivity over prudence. For example, if a reactor engaged in the production of plutonium for nuclear weapons became damaged, requiring repairs that would, if handled safely, keep it off-line for a year or more, then workers were sent in to repair it by hand, and to do so unprotected. Such an event occurred in June 1948, according to a September 1999 article in the *Bulletin of the Atomic Scientists*, and it involved the replacement of the entire reactor core—by hand—a process that led to "huge doses of radiation" to the personnel involved. But the repairs were completed within two months.

Chelyabinsk-65 was also the site of the largest accident in nuclear history prior to the 1986 accident at Chernobyl. In September 1957 a steel tank holding liquid nuclear waste exploded, spreading radiation over an area of 23,000 square kilometers, or approximately 9,000 square miles, and affecting approximately a quarter of a million people, ten thousand of whom had to be permanently evacuated from their homes. As was the case at many other links in the nuclear weapons infrastructural chain, the plutonium and uranium processing at Chelyabinsk-65 was undertaken with little regard for the safe storage of waste. Indeed, for much of the complex's early life, waste generated was simply dumped into nearby rivers and lakes.

Disregard for Safe Waste Disposal

The River Techa was the destination for much of this waste, and radiation from Chelyabinsk-65 has been found in waters as far away as the Arctic Ocean, a

The Union of Soviet Socialist Republics

The Union of Soviet Socialist Republics, or the Soviet Union, was the world's first Communist state, existing from 1922 to 1991. It was a one-party socialist regime, with the decisions of the ruling Communist party carried out by an executive committee and policymaking body. The country's Communist era began with an immediate and radical program to establish a "dictatorship of the proletariat"—the proletariat being the class of workers. This would serve as a transitional state between the formerly capitalist society—whereby the means of production are controlled by a few for their own enrichment, according to Communist ideology—to a classless society where all shared a nation's resources equally.

The original union comprised the Russian Soviet Federative Socialist Republic, Ukraine, Belarus, and the Transcaucasus (Georgia, Armenia, and Azerbaijan), and over the next twenty years it would add—most often by force—several other constituent republics in Central Asia and the Baltic nations of Latvia, Lithuania, and Estonia. Soviet constitutions evolved to protect its citizens, ensuring their rights to work and to an education, their medical care, housing needs, and old-age pensions. Civil liberties such as freedom of speech, religion, and of assembly were protected by the Constitution—so long as they did not infringe upon the goals

thousand miles to the north. Closer to home the Techa represented the drinking water supply for approximately 125,000 people: when it became public knowledge that the water was highly radioactive the Soviet government resettled some 7,000 of them. Greenpeace estimates, however, that perhaps 8,000 residents who drew their water from the Techa have died of radiation-induced illnesses.

Similarly, another repository for Chelyabinsk-65's waste has the dubious distinction today of being the most radioactively polluted spot on the planet. For decades liquid and solid waste containing extremely high levels of radioactivity were dumped into Lake Karachay, close to Chelyabinsk-65. In 1967 the lake dried up and of the state or tenets of the Communist Party.

As one of the world's two superpowers for much of the twentieth century, the Soviet Union played a decisive role in nearly all major world events and social developments, and though it never entered into direct military engagement with the United States, surrogate battles were played out in Korea, Vietnam, Africa, Latin America, and the Caribbean. Soviet influence on the political life of Eastern Europe remained a difficult legacy more than a decade after Soviet dissolution, as each of the newly independent nations struggled to join an international community of democratic, free-market states. Governments strained to achieve a multiparty political life given the threat posed by right-wing or even still-active Communist elements within their populace.

What may be the Soviet Union's greatest legacy was the rapid transformation of a largely agrarian, near-medieval society into one of the most heavily industrialized, literate, and scientifically advanced nations in the world within just a few short decades—an achievement accomplished by the sheer force and power of a party leadership who recognized that their authority and the security of their state was dependent entirely on economic might, not ideological right.

winds spread highly radioactive dust across a wide area, affecting tens of thousands of people both directly, as the dust was inhaled or ingested, and indirectly, as it contaminated their livestock and crops. The solution to the problem was typically Soviet: the entire lake-bed was sealed with concrete, a process not completed until the late 1990s.

The situation at Chelyabinsk-65 was not unique. Mismanagement of waste and disregard for safety were common characteristics at most of the nuclear production centers in the Soviet Union. Of course, the glaring question stands out: why was there such

> " In Soviet society information was an extraordinarily controlled commodity.

recklessness in the nuclear weapons program? The answer to that question is complex and consists of several aspects. First and foremost is the national security issue: the creation and maintenance of a nuclear arsenal comparable to that of the United States was seen by the Soviet leadership as the central guarantee of security during the Cold War. In essence, environmental or health problems were accepted as trade-offs in the creation, expansion, and maintenance of that nuclear arsenal. Second, in Soviet society information was an extraordinarily controlled commodity.

Events such as the accidents at Chelyabinsk that undermined the superiority of communism, or the infallibility of the Communist Party of the Soviet Union, were suppressed as a matter of course. Indeed, the initial response of the Soviet leadership to the Chernobyl disaster of April 1986 was to "hush it up," to deny that anything serious had happened. It was only when radioactivity was detected in large quantities in northern and western Europe and European experts confronted the Soviet Union with this incontrovertible proof that the true story became known.

Third, a balanced nuclear infrastructure, whether military or civilian, requires the creation of a so-called "complete cycle," involving the production, the processing, *and* the storage and disposal of by-products and waste. The storage and disposal of nuclear waste is, unfortunately, expensive; it is also crucial for environmental and human health. The Soviet economy could not encompass all three parts of the cycle, and concentrated primarily on weapons production. Whatever funds were left over were applied to the third leg of the cycle. They were not sufficient to do the job. As will be seen, the nuclear problem piled up as the Cold War matured and ended, to the extent that the states that succeeded the Soviet Union simply cannot deal with the problem without external aid in massive amounts.

Civilian Application of Nuclear Energy

The Soviet Union laid claim to the first civilian nuclear power station, which became operational at Obninsk, a small city in western Russia, in 1954. This was, however, a reactor primarily involved in the production of nuclear fuel for atomic weaponry, and it was not until the late 1960s that civilian applications of nuclear power began to expand in the Soviet Union. The country was extraordinarily gifted in terms of its fossil fuel resources, and so the rapid expansion of the nuclear power infrastructure after 1970 is somewhat difficult to explain in purely economic terms. There is no doubt, however, that the cutting-edge technology represented by nuclear power was attractive to the Soviet leadership.

During the Cold War, technological prowess was an important indicator of the strength of the communist system, and the broad application of nuclear power could, in the estimation of the Soviet leadership under Leonid Brezhnev (1906–1982) and his immediate successors, demonstrate the superiority of the USSR in the world arena. Nuclear energy could also solve a problem confronting the Soviet economy in the 1970s. Although fossil fuel reserves remained vast, the extraction of coal, oil, and natural gas became increasingly concentrated in Siberia—a harsh, difficult, and therefore expensive environment in which to operate. The net costs of energy in the USSR began to rise in the late 1960s and 1970s and the establishment of a nuclear power grid promised to offset these rising costs to some extent.

> Despite the fact that the RBMK [nuclear reactor] formed the basis of . . . rapid expansion in the 1970s and early 1980s, it was nevertheless a profoundly flawed design.

Soviet nuclear power reactors were developed along two main lines. The first of these, a direct outgrowth of the reactors used by the military for the production of weapons-grade uranium and plutonium, was a simple

Reactors like the one at Chernobyl— including this one in Lithuania—were built throughout the former Soviet Union in order to develop the Soviet nuclear energy program. (AFP/Getty Images.)

type in which the nuclear reaction is "moderated" or controlled by graphite (the same material found in so-called "lead" pencils). The graphite, formed into rods that can be inserted into or withdrawn from the reactor's core, absorbs neutrons produced during the nuclear reaction. The amount of neutrons available governs the rate of the reaction and therefore the amount of power generated: as the rods are inserted, the reaction slows and generates less power, as they are withdrawn the reaction increases and generates more power.

Following experiments conducted at Obninsk in the 1950s and at the Beloyarsk station at Shevchenko (now Aqtau, a town in southwestern Kazakhstan) in the 1960s with graphite-moderated reactors, known by their Russian acronym RBMK, scaled-up commercial RBMK-based power stations were constructed at several sites around the western USSR in the 1970s. Another, larger

RBMK plant became operational at Ignalina in Lithuania in 1983, and others were on the drawing board or under construction in the early 1980s.

Despite the fact that the RBMK formed the basis of this rapid expansion in the 1970s and early 1980s, it was nevertheless a profoundly flawed design. It became unstable when generating low levels of power, being prone to sudden "spikes" of energy that could raise the temperature within the reactor and, if unchecked, lead to a meltdown of the core—the so-called "China Syndrome" of popular imagination. Documents released since the collapse of the Soviet Union make it clear that the RBMK's design flaws were well known to both engineers and planners, yet RBMKs were not fitted with a secondary, reinforced concrete containment structure common in Western designs. That such domes were not constructed is again a consequence of economics: the main goal was the construction and operation of the reactor *itself*; "expensive" safety features were considered secondary in the design.

The WER Reactor

The other major Soviet reactor type was based on a pressurized-water design that employed water rather than graphite as the reaction moderator. Known as the WER, this type was widely produced in the 1970s and 1980s, with reactors being constructed in Ukraine, Armenia, Russia, and in satellite states in Eastern Europe. In all, more than fifty WERs were constructed during the Soviet period.

Though inherently safer than the RBMK design, WERs nevertheless fall far short of western safety standards. Most lack secondary containment structures and they have poor emergency shutdown facilities. A measure of their unacceptability may be seen in the fact that, upon German unification in 1990, West German nuclear specialists inspected and then hurriedly shut down all five Soviet-designed WERs that had been operating on East German soil. Other Eastern European countries that still operate WERs have come under heavy pressure from the western community since 1989 to shut down their reactors for the same reason.

Despite safety questions the WER design was nevertheless seen as the centerpiece of Soviet nuclear power in the foreseeable future. Indeed, in the 1980s the future looked bright for the Soviet nuclear industry. New plants, based on WER reactors, were being commissioned throughout the Soviet bloc, and dozens more were under construction or on the drawing board. Rosy projections foresaw nuclear power accounting for almost one-third of the Soviet Union's electrical generating capacity by the year 2000, and over half of the capacity for East European satellite states such as Hungary, Bulgaria, and Czechoslovakia. These projections and indeed the entire Soviet nuclear industry were thrown into chaos by the catastrophic accident at the No. 4 reactor of the Chernobyl nuclear power plant on 26 April 1986. Many reactors under construction were suspended indefinitely whilst those on the drawing board were cancelled outright. Other plants underwent extensive modifications that improved their safety to a certain degree but not to western standards.

The Chernobyl accident had a profound impact on Soviet society. Many commentators agree that the magnitude of the event undermined the authority of the Communist Party (under whose leadership such calamities were not supposed to happen). It unleashed long-simmering bitterness among the constituent republics of the Soviet Union—especially in Ukraine, on whose soil the accident occurred—against Moscow. It awakened an environmental consciousness among Soviet citizens, and it highlighted general economic and social ills in the Soviet Union. There is no doubt that Chernobyl forced a dramatic shift in [general secretary of the Communist

Party] Mikhail Gorbachev's policies of glasnost [government "openness"] and perestroika [political & economic reform], pushing them much further, and much faster, than Gorbachev and his reformist allies had intended. It is perhaps too much to claim, as some commentators have done, that Chernobyl "caused" the collapse of the Soviet Union. Still, it is important not to underestimate its impact either.

> *Chernobyl gave the Soviet people a basis upon which they could criticize other broad failures of the communist system.*

Chernobyl gave the Soviet people a basis upon which they could criticize other broad failures of the communist system. It was *that* attack upon its legitimacy that the Communist Party of the Soviet Union was unable to weather. Indeed, a last desperate attempt by communist hard-liners to "turn the clock back" on reform by ousting Gorbachev in August 1991 collapsed into farce as the army, the secret police, and the common citizenry simply refused to acquiesce in the face of this tawdry bid for power. Once the party itself was stripped of authority in real terms, the dissolution of the Soviet Union itself—which had been held together in large part by the threat of force or its application—was inevitable.

The Nuclear Hangover

Ironically, the period immediately after the collapse of the Soviet Union was, relatively speaking, quite kind to the nuclear industry there. The 1990s were marked by sharp declines in the output of fossil fuels (crude oil production fell by almost half between 1988 and 1995, for example), as the energy sector struggled in times of economic chaos and deep cash shortages. Massive debts accrued to the energy sector as a whole, as consumers—from individual households to large industrial complexes—simply stopped paying their power bills. To a certain extent the nuclear industry was insulated from the most serious economic hardships by foreign aid, especially from the United States and, though shrunken from its high point in the mid-1980s, it still produced over 11 percent of Russia's electrical power in 1995 and output actually increased, albeit slowly, as the 1990s progressed.

Not surprisingly this performance led to the nuclear industry being hailed domestically as the answer to Russia's energy problems. In 1992 the Russian nuclear power industry (Rosenergoatom) announced that reactors whose construction had been suspended in the aftermath of Chernobyl would be completed and new reactors brought on line as well. However, the upbeat projections failed to take account of economic reality: Russia simply did not have the economic wherewithal to pay for such an expansion, and in the end only one of the long list of reactors was completed, at the Balakovo power station.

In other successor states of the Soviet Union the nuclear energy situation was, and remains, more complex. Ukraine, under heavy pressure to close the remaining three reactors at the Chernobyl plant, engaged in a long, difficult series of negotiations with the international community for aid to do so, and to construct coal-fired plants to replace Chernobyl's generating capacity. It took almost a decade and a $3.2 billion international pledge, but the last reactor at Chernobyl was finally shut down in December 2000. The problem facing Ukraine, Lithuania, and Armenia—states that had inherited nuclear power plants from the Soviet period—is that, relatively speaking, those plants generate much more of the state's electrical power than is the case in Russia.

Ukraine relies on its 13 remaining nuclear power stations for about one-third of the country's electricity; Lithuania's old and unsafe Ignalina plant accounts for about three-quarters of that state's electrical capacity; and the Metsamor plant in Armenia meets approximately 40 percent of the country's electricity requirements.

Thus, shutting down the reactors is not a straightforward proposition: doing so will lead to a serious reduction in energy output, with the likelihood of economic instability to follow. Bilateral negotiations have therefore focused on replacing that energy shortfall, either through the building of fossil-fuel plants or through energy imports financed by Western credits.

Further compounding the nuclear power problem in these successor states is that none of them possess significant fuel reprocessing or waste storage facilities on their territory. During the Soviet period, as we have seen, those complexes were located on Russian soil; after the collapse of the Soviet Union other successor states had to conclude not always equitable agreements for their use. In any case, the reprocessing and storage facilities inherited by Russia were in an appalling state in their own right.

Soviet Secrecy in the Face of Calamity

Celestine Bohlen

The following article originally appeared in the *Washington Post* on April 29, 1986, three days after the accident at Chernobyl. All of the early reporting on this catastrophe was based on a combination of guesswork and the very brief news reports released by the Telegraph Agency of the Soviet Union (abbreviated as "Tass"). Tass was the Soviet agency that dictated what information could be made available to newspapers, radio stations, and television stations in the Soviet Union. Prior to these first reports, even Soviets living in nearby Kiev (60 miles south of the reactor) were largely unaware there was a problem at the reactor. Western officials speculated that the death toll most have been extremely high to warrant any reporting at all in the Soviet Union, which had previously covered up several very severe nuclear accidents. As it turned out, the initial death toll from the accident (several dozen people) was several orders of magnitude lower than Western experts had suspected.

The Soviet Union said tonight that an accident at a major nuclear power plant in the Ukraine had damaged a reactor and caused unspecified casualties. The unexplained accident also sent a radioactive cloud hundreds of miles over Scandinavia.

The announcement, unusual for the Soviet Union, which rarely publicizes disasters, came several hours after four Scandinavian countries had reported detecting abnormally high levels of radioactivity in their atmosphere and Sweden's ambassador to Moscow began questioning Soviet officials.

The Soviet statement did not say whether there were deaths in the accident, which the news agency Tass said was at the Chernobyl power plant, 60 miles north of

AREAS CONTAMINATED BY RADIATION FROM CHERNOBYL

Taken from: Michelle Carter, *Children of Chernobyl*, 1993.

Kiev. It said only that "measures are being undertaken to eliminate the consequences of the accident. Aid is being given to those affected."

Residents of Kiev told United Press International [UPI] by telephone that all bus service there had been stopped so the vehicles could be used to evacuate those in the disaster area. They said, however, that they had no information about casualties and had heard no explosion.

The Tass statement, read on the television evening news, said one of the plant's atomic reactors was damaged and "a government commission has been set up" to investigate it. This was seen by western diplomats as an indication of high-level concern.

Western Powers Left Guessing

Some western diplomats here speculated that because of the proximity to Kiev, a city of 2.3 million people, and the unusual public announcement, there may have been a high death toll.

Officials in Sweden, where radio-activity was detected in the air, soil and tree leaves, said that the amount reaching that country was well above normal, but presented no immediate threat to the population.

> The radioactive cloud, traveling over the Arctic, could reach the West Coast of the United States in five or six days.

Denmark, Finland and Norway also reported unusual radioactivity, with high readings coming from islands in the Baltic Sea.

Sweden said that it is seeking "detailed information" from Soviet authorities about the accident, so that it can take precautionary measures if the contamination can be expected to continue or increase.

Swedish Energy Minister Birgitta Dahl said it was "unacceptable" that Swedish authorities and others outside the Soviet Union had been given no notification.

Sweden would demand that the entire Soviet civilian nuclear program be made subject to international inspections, she added.

The radioactive cloud, traveling over the Arctic, could reach the West Coast of the United States in five or six days, a spokesman for the Environmental Protection Agency's Radiation Alert Network told United Press International. The spokesman said that until the agency could get a radiation-level reading, there was no way of knowing what effect the fallout could have in the United States. [White House spokesman Edward Djerejian said that the accident "must be very serious if the Soviets talk about it."]

One western diplomat said the Soviet statement "almost certainly indicated that the death toll was high," UPI reported. Another said that, because of the wording of the statement, "it is not unreasonable to speculate about deaths."

The Soviets did not say when the accident occurred, but Scandinavian experts said that their trackings and wind patterns indicated that it had happened early in the weekend.

A later Tass story called the accident "the first one in the Soviet Union"—a description disputed by U.S. and other western authorities—and listed what it said were similar nuclear plant accidents in other countries, including the United States.

> The Soviet Union has traditionally provided little information—and then only belatedly—on accidents and natural disasters of all kinds, particularly in sensitive areas such as nuclear power.

Soviet History of Concealing Mishaps

Although the official Soviet record shows no previous accidents here, there have been reports of several, of which the most serious was an alleged explosion at a remote plutonium processing plant in the Urals in 1957, reported by former Soviet scientist Zhores Medvedev

Due to the Soviet embrace of secrecy, many speculated a large death toll, and the worst to come, for the surrounding countries at Chernobyl. (Scott Peterson/Liason/Getty Images.)

and by a 1980 study compiled by the Oak Ridge National Laboratory in Tennessee.

Medvedev, who now lives in London, wrote that an explosion of nuclear waste near the city of Kyshtym killed and injured thousands of people. The area has been closed since the time of the reported disaster, and some of the towns have been removed from Soviet maps.

Unofficial sources have reported other events, such as damage in 1981 to a steam generator at a plant in Rovno, also in the Ukraine. In 1982, a Soviet magazine appeared to confirm a leak from the power plant in Leningrad, which raised radiation levels in the Gulf of Finland and the Baltic Sea.

Clearly anticipating western news accounts scrutinizing the safety record of the Soviet nuclear power industry, Tass described what it called "the dangerous situation" at U.S. nuclear plants, which it said was due to "the poor quality of reactors" and lax safety measures.

The Soviet Union has traditionally provided little information—and then only belatedly—on accidents and natural disasters of all kinds, particularly in sensitive areas such as nuclear power.

Asked about safety on a television program last winter, Anatoly Mayorets, minister of power and electrification, said that "unequivocally" nuclear energy is "ecologically the purest source of electricity" for both workers and the environment.

Many Soviet nuclear plants are built close to centers of population.

The promptness of tonight's disclosure of the Chernobyl accident, observers said, could reflect either a new trend toward openness or response to the concern raised in Scandinavia by the radioactive cloud.

Since Mikhail Gorbachev became the Soviet leader in March 1985, the Soviet press has been urged to treat shortcomings, failures, problems, even calamities, with more candor.

After the statement on the 9 P.M. news—which is viewed by millions of Soviet citizens—a formal request for additonal information was made to the Soviet Foreign Ministry by the Swedish Embassy, which hopes to get some answers [soon].

Without full and official data, it is difficult, if not impossible, to track the true safety record in the Soviet nuclear program.

Importance of Nuclear Power in USSR

For the first time in history, the Soviets agreed [in 1985] to allow international inspectors to visit two nuclear power plants. Inspectors from the Vienna-based International Atomic Energy Agency visited the plants [in] summer [of 1985], including one in Voronezh, in central Russia.

The Soviet Union now has 15 atomic power plants, with more than 30 reactors. Its nuclear power program, now gearing up for a major push, is one of the world's largest, ranking behind only the United States and France in capacity.

Nuclear power now supplies about 9 percent of the country's electricity needs, but that dependence is to be pushed up to about 19 percent by 1990, and 30 percent by 2000, according to recently adopted plans.

Dependence on nuclear energy is particularly important in the European part of the Soviet Union, where there are few remaining natural energy resources and a concentration of industry.

The current five-year plan calls for nuclear energy production to increase from 170 billion kilowatt hours in 1985 to about 370 billion in 1990.

Previous five-year plans have set ambitious goals for the nuclear power program that have not been met. A major problem has been the production of standardized 1,000 megawatt units, which was slowed down by problems at the giant Atommash facility in Volgadonsk.

The Chernobyl plant, reportedly situated near the town on the Pripyat River, is made up of four reactors, of which the most recent went into operation [in 1983]. All four reactors at Chernobyl are 1,000 megawatts, the basic Soviet model.

The Soviet Myth of Safety

Grigori Medvedev

Grigori Medvedev was chief engineer during the Chernobyl nuclear facility's construction in the 1970s. His book *The Truth About Chernobyl* (published in 1989, just as European communism was showing signs of crumbling, but prior to the fall of the Soviet Union) is the result of his detailed investigation of the accident.

In the following viewpoint, drawn from his book, Medvedev argues that an accident like the meltdown at Chernobyl was inevitable not because of flaws in the reactor's design (although he readily acknowledges these), but because of decades of government assurances that atomic energy was safer and cleaner than fossil fuels. Government propaganda, coupled with the systematic censoring of reports of any Soviet or international nuclear mishap, led the Soviet people to disregard the possibility of any sort of dangerous accident and thus terribly compounded the impact of the frequent radioactive mishaps.

SOURCE. Grigori Medvedev, *The Truth About Chernobyl*. Cambridge, MA: Basic Books, 1991. English Translation copyright © 1991 by Basic Books, Inc. Original edition copyright © 1989 by VAAP, Moscou. Reprinted by permission of Basic Books, a member of Perseus Books.

"The loss of the [U.S. space shuttle] *Challenger* crew [on January 23, 1986] and the accident at the Chernobyl nuclear power station have heightened our sense of alarm and been a cruel reminder that mankind is still trying to come to grips with the fantastic, powerful forces which it has itself brought into being, and is still only learning to use them for the sake of progress," said [the last Soviet leader] Mikhail Sergeyevich Gorbachev in his statement on Soviet Central TV on 18 August 1986.

> The ordinary citizen was made to believe that the peaceful atom was virtually a panacea and the ultimate in genuine safety, ecological cleanliness, and reliability.

This exceedingly sober assessment of the peaceful uses of nuclear energy was the first of its kind in the thirty-five years of the development of nuclear power in the Soviet Union. The Soviet leader's words were unquestionably a sign of the times, and of the wind of purifying truth and change which has swept so powerfully over our country [Russia].

Even so, in order to learn the lessons of the past, we must remember that throughout an entire three and a half decades, in the press and on radio and television, our scientists have repeatedly told the general public the exact opposite. The ordinary citizen was made to believe that the peaceful atom was virtually a panacea and the ultimate in genuine safety, ecological cleanliness, and reliability. The whole subject of the safety of nuclear power stations generated much ecstatic enthusiasm.

Photo on next page: The Soviet populace was poorly informed of the dangers and harm from the radioactive blast at the Chernobyl nuclear power station. Many people were sickened or killed by the radiation, and large populated cities were abandoned. (Daniel Berehulak/Getty Images.)

Cheerful Optimism

In 1980, in the monthly magazine *Ogonyok*, Academician M. A. Styrikovich exclaimed, "Nuclear power stations are like stars that shine all day long! We shall sow them all over the land. They are perfectly safe!" And that is precisely what they did.

N.M. Sinev, deputy head of the State Committee on the Utilization of Nuclear Energy, used a homespun image to explain matters to the general reader: "Nuclear reactors are regular furnaces, and the operators who run them are stokers." He thus neatly equated nuclear reactors with ordinary steam boilers and nuclear station operators with stokers who shovel coal into a furnace.

This was in every respect a convenient position to take. First of all, it reassured the public; and secondly, it made it possible to pay the staff of nuclear power stations the same wages as workers at thermal power stations, and in a number of cases even less. Nuclear energy was cheap and straightforward, so the pay could be lower. By the early 1980s the wages at thermal power stations had exceeded those paid to operators at nuclear power stations.

> Radioactive exposure of this sort occurred, virtually without interruption, for almost fifteen years.

But let us continue to scrutinize the cheerfully optimistic assertions about the complete safety of nuclear power stations.

"The waste products of nuclear power, which are potentially extremely dangerous, are so compact that they can be stored in places isolated from the environment," according to the director of the Physico-Energy Institute, O.D. Kazachkovsky, writing in *Pravda* [the official Soviet newspaper] on 25 July 1984. In actual fact, at the time of the Chernobyl explosion, it turned out that there was nowhere to deposit the spent nuclear fuel. In the previous few decades, no storage facilities for spent nuclear fuel had been built; and one had to be built next to the damaged reactor, in a highly radioactive environment, thus exposing construction and installation crews to severe doses of radiation.

"We live in a nuclear age. Nuclear power stations have proved convenient and reliable in operation. Nuclear reactors are preparing to take on the task of heating cit-ies and built-up areas," O.D. Kazachkovsky wrote in that same issue of *Pravda*, while forgetting to say that nuclear thermal power stations would be erected near major cities.

One month later, Academician Aleksandr Yefimovich Sheidlin declared in *Literaturnaya Gazeta*, "We were delighted to hear of a remarkable achievement—the start-up of No. 4 reactor, generating one million kilo-watts of electricity, at the V.I. Lenin nuclear power sta-tion, Chernobyl."

One wonders whether the academician's heart missed a beat when he wrote those words, as it was precisely No. 4 reactor that was destined to explode so resonantly—truly a bolt from the blue sky of guaranteed safety at nuclear power stations.

On another occasion, when a correspondent remarked that the expanded construction of nuclear power stations might alarm the general public, the academician replied, "People can be very emotional about these things. The nuclear power stations in our country are perfectly safe for the populations of surrounding areas. There is quite simply nothing to worry about."

A Systemic Disregard for Safety

The chairman of the Soviet Union State Committee on the Use of Nuclear Energy, A.M. Petrosyants, played a major role in advertising the safety of nuclear power sta-tions. In his *From Scientific Search to Nuclear Industry*, written fourteen years before the Chernobyl explosion, he wrote:

> It must be acknowledged that nuclear energy has a bril-liant future. Nuclear energy has definite advantages over conventional energy. Nuclear power stations are entirely independent of sources of raw materials (uranium mines), because nuclear fuel is very compact and can be

kept in use for a very long time. Nuclear power stations hold great promise for the use of powerful reactors.

The reassuring conclusion he then reached was that nuclear power stations are clean sources of energy which do not add to environmental pollution.

Turning then to the question of the extent to which nuclear power was to be developed, and its status beyond the year 2000, Petrosyants focused mainly on the adequacy of stockpiles of uranium ore, leaving completely aside the question of the safety of an extensive network of nuclear power stations located in the most densely populated regions of the European part of the Soviet Union. "The main issue in nuclear energy is how to make the most rational use of the miraculous property of nuclear fuel," he emphasized in that same book. And he was concerned primarily not with safety at nuclear power stations but with the rational use of nuclear fuel. He went on to say:

> The continuing skepticism and distrust felt toward nuclear power stations are caused by exaggerated fear of the radiation danger to the personnel working at the station and, in particular, to the surrounding population.
>
> The operation of nuclear power stations in the Soviet Union and abroad, including the United States, Britain, France, Canada, Italy, Japan, the German Democratic Republic and the Federal Republic of Germany shows that they work with complete safety, provided that the established regimes and the necessary rules are observed. Moreover, one could argue about whether nuclear or coal-fired power stations are more harmful for human beings and the environment.

At this point for some reason, Petrosyants failed to note that thermal power stations can run not only on coal and oil (and that in any case such pollution is local in character and far from lethal) but also on gaseous fuel, vast quantities of which are extracted in the Soviet Union and, as is well-known, transported to a number of destinations, including Western Europe. The conversion of the thermal power stations of the European part of the country to gaseous fuel could completely eliminate the problem of pollution from ash and sulfuric anhydride. Yet Petrosyants managed to turn that problem upside down, too, by devoting a whole chapter of his book to the question of environmental pollution from coal-fired thermal power stations, while remaining silent about actual instances of environmental pollution from nuclear power stations, with which he must have been familiar. This was no accidental omission. It was intended to steer the reader toward an optimistic conclusion: "The above-mentioned data on the favorable radiation situation within the vicinity of the Novo-Voronezh and Byeloyarsk nuclear power stations are typical for all the nuclear power stations in the Soviet Union. That same favorable radiation situation is also characteristic of the nuclear power stations of other countries," he concluded, in a display of corporate solidarity with the nuclear industry in foreign countries.

> 'Science requires victims.'

Reactor Maintenance and Safety Problems

At the same time, Petrosyants must have known that ever since it was first brought on-line in 1964, the first single-loop reactor at the Byeloyarsk nuclear power station had repeatedly broken down: the uranium fuel assemblies had behaved in a most capricious manner; and while repairing them, the staff were exposed to heavy doses of radiation. Radioactive exposure of this sort occurred, virtually without interruption, for almost fifteen years. In 1977, in the second reactor at that same station, also with a single-loop design, 50 percent of the nuclear reactor's fuel assemblies melted down. Repairs lasted one year. The personnel of the Byeloyarsk nuclear power station were quickly exposed to severe doses of radiation, and people had to be brought in from other nuclear power stations to perform hazardous repair work. He also must have been aware that in the town of Melekess, in the Ulyanovsk region, highly radioactive waste was being dumped in fissures far underground; that the British nuclear reactors at Windscale, Winfrith, and Dounreay had been discharging radioactive water into the Irish Sea since the 1950s (and they still are [as of 1989]). The list of such facts could be continued. I shall merely note that, at the Moscow press conference on the Chernobyl tragedy on 6 May 1986, Petrosyants shocked a great many people with the following remark: "Science requires victims." That is something one cannot forget.

Now, some more pronouncements on the development of nuclear energy.

> The optimistic forecasts and assurances on the part of scientists were, of course, never shared by the operators of nuclear [power] plants.

Obstacles could naturally be expected during the development of such a new industrial sector. In his *I.V. Kurchatov and Nuclear Power*, Y.V. Sivintsev, who like Kurchatov [head of the Soviet atomic bomb project during World War II] was also an advocate of nuclear power, included some interesting reminiscences about earlier efforts to win public acceptance for the notion of the "peaceful atom," and about the difficulties encountered:

Opponents of nuclear power abroad and in this country sometimes score "victories" in their fight against innovation. The most widely publicized of these was the cancelation of the nuclear power station in Austria, which was decided on shortly after a strident anti-nuclear campaign. Western journalists were quick to christen that plant "a billion-dollar mausoleum." The development of nuclear power in the Soviet Union has also had to surmount certain difficulties. In the late 1950s, the advocates of traditional forms of energy prepared the decision of the Communist Party Central Committee and the Council of Ministers of the Soviet Union for halting construction of the Novo-Voronezh nuclear power station and building in its place a conventional thermal power station; moreover, they came very close to having that decision implemented. The main justification was that nuclear power stations were uneconomical at the time. On hearing of this, Kurchatov dropped everything, went to the Kremlin [the seat of Soviet government], and managed to arrange for a new meeting of the senior officials; after a heated discussion with the skeptics, he persuaded the authorities to uphold their previous decisions about the construction of nuclear power stations. One of the secretaries of the CPSU [Communist Party of the Soviet Union] Central Committee then asked him, "What are we going to get?" Kurchatov replied, "Nothing! For some thirty years it's going to be an expensive experiment." Nonetheless, he got his way. It is easy to understand why some of us used terms like *nuclear reactor, human tank*, and even *bomb* to describe him.

The optimistic forecasts and assurances on the part of scientists were, of course, never shared by the operators of nuclear plants, who had to deal with the peaceful atom directly, every day, at their place of work and not in the comfort of some quiet office or laboratory. Throughout all those years, information about breakdowns and mishaps at nuclear power stations was rigorously sifted by the extremely cautious ministries, which divulged only what senior policymakers deemed it necessary to publish. I well recall a landmark event of those days—the Three Mile Island accident [a partial core meltdown of

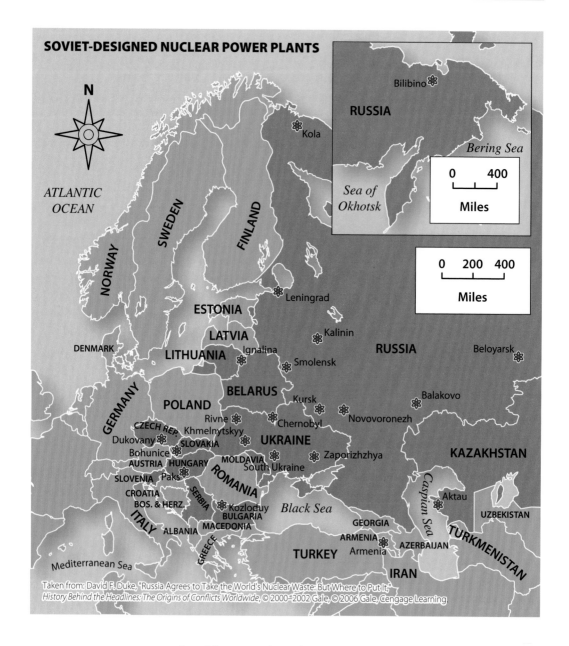

SOVIET-DESIGNED NUCLEAR POWER PLANTS

Taken from: David F. Duke, "Russia Agrees to Take the World's Nuclear Waste: But Where to Put It,"
History Behind the Headlines: The Origins of Conflicts Worldwide, © 2000–2002 Gale, © 2006 Gale, Cengage Learning.

the Three Mile Island Nuclear Generating Station in Pennsylvania] on 28 March 1979, which struck the first serious blow against nuclear power and, in the minds of many but not all, dispelled illusions about the safety of nuclear power stations.

Censoring Reports on Nuclear Accidents

At the time I was a section chief in Soyuzatomenergo, the department of the Soviet Ministry of Energy and Electrification which operates nuclear power stations, and I remember how I and my colleagues reacted to that distressing event. Having worked for many years before in the assembly, maintenance, and operation of nuclear power stations, and realizing from firsthand experience that safety at such plants was literally on the razor's edge or a hair's breadth away from breakdown or disaster, we said at the time, "It had to happen sooner or later. Something like that could happen here, too."

> Sober reminders of the possible environmental hazards of nuclear power stations were treated as an attack on the authority of science.

But neither I nor people who had worked previously at nuclear power stations were fully informed about the accident. A detailed account of events in Pennsylvania was provided in the *Information Sheet*, which was distributed to the heads of major government departments and their deputies. The question is: Why was there such a need for secrecy in connection with an accident the whole world knew about? After all, knowledge of negative experiences, if promptly transmitted, can help guarantee that the same mistakes are not repeated. In those days, however, the custom was to keep negative information exclusively for the most senior leaders, while censored versions were passed on to those lower down. Yet even those censored versions gave rise to depressing thoughts about the insidious nature of radiation, should it, despite all precautions, actually escape, and also about the need to make the general public aware of those problems. But in those days it was simply impossible to organize that kind of educational effort, as it would have clashed with the official line about the complete safety of nuclear power stations.

Then, deciding to go it alone, I wrote four short stories about the way people live and work at nuclear power stations. Their titles were: "The Operators," "The Expert Opinion," "The Reactor," and "A Nuclear Tan." When I tried to get them into print, however, the publishers replied, "What do you mean? Academicians are always writing that Soviet nuclear power stations are perfectly safe. Academician Kirillin even intends to start a garden right next to a nuclear power station—and you're writing all this stuff! In the West this kind of thing could happen, but not here!" The senior editor of a leading monthly journal, after praising one of the short stories, even said, "If this had happened in the West, then we would have published it."

Even so, I did manage to get one of the short stories— "The Operators"—published in that journal in 1981. I am glad that I succeeded in warning at least those who managed to read it.

Those were, however, what we call the "stagnant years," when things moved at their own sluggish pace, so I shall not anticipate events. After all, everything destined to happen did actually happen. Scientific circles remained calm and unruffled. Sober reminders of the possible environmental hazards of nuclear power stations were treated as an attack on the authority of science.

Shaken Confidence

In 1974, at the annual general meeting of the Soviet Academy of Sciences, Academician A.P. Aleksandrov said in particular, "Our critics claim that nuclear power is dangerous and poses the threat of radioactive contamination of the environment. But what about a nuclear war, comrades? What kind of contamination would occur then?"

The logic behind this remark is truly astounding.

Ten years later, at a meeting of the active party members in the Soviet Ministry of Energy, one year before

Chernobyl, the same A.P. Aleksandrov commented, on a melancholy note, "Fate has been kind to us, comrades, in that we haven't had a Pennsylvania of our own. Yes, I mean it."

This shows a striking evolution in the thinking of the president of the Soviet Academy of Sciences. Ten years, of course, is a long time, and Aleksandrov can certainly be credited with anticipating the onset of disaster. A great deal had been going on in the nuclear industry: some grave irregularities and breakdowns had occurred; there had been an unprecedented rise in generating capacity; pressures associated with prestige projects had also increased; and the sense of responsibility of those working in the nuclear power industry was clearly beginning to slacken. One wonders, of course, how they could be expected to show a keen sense of responsibility, when at the nuclear power stations themselves everything was apparently so simple and safe.

It was approximately during those same years that changes began to occur in the personnel running the nuclear power stations, as the shortage of operators suddenly grew acute. Those seeking such employment had previously been, for the most part, real enthusiasts, with a profound passion for nuclear energy; whereas now all kinds of people were pouring in. Of course, they were attracted primarily not by the pay, which was not particularly good, but by the lure of prestige. There were people who had earned good money in some other field but had not yet held posts in the nuclear industry. After all, for many years everyone had been saying it was safe! So what are we waiting for? Out of the way, you nuclear experts! Step aside and make room at the important nuclear pie for brothers-in-law and the well connected! And the nuclear experts were shoved out of the way.

> "Nuclear experts were shoved out of the way.

An Economic Catastrophe

Richard L. Hudson

Richard L. Hudson is a science journalist who worked for the *Wall Street Journal* for two decades, rising from staff reporter to managing editor of the *Journal*'s European edition. In 2006 he teamed up with famed mathematician Benoit Mandelbrot to write a book exploring applications of fractal geometry in finance.

In the following article—written by Hudson in 1990 when he was still a staff reporter with the *Journal*—he examines the spiraling costs associated with the Chernobyl accident, from cleanup, to the costs of lost farmland and increased energy expenses. He bases his article on a report that came to light as part of public debates on increasing the budget for Ukrainian cleanup efforts. In the report, a Soviet nuclear-industry economist estimated that the total cost of the accident would be roughly twenty times greater than originally estimated. A year-and-a-half after this report was made public, the Soviet Union collapsed.

SOURCE. Richard L. Hudson, "Cost of Chernobyl Nuclear Disaster Soars in New Study—1986 Reactor Accident Dwarfs Other Soviet Peacetime Catastrophes," *The Wall Street Journal*, March 29, 1990, p. A8. Copyright © 1990 by Dow Jones & Company. Republished with permission of Wall Street Journal, conveyed through Copyright Clearance Center, Inc.

A new Soviet study concludes that continuing economic fallout from the Chernobyl nuclear accident may cost 20 times more than Moscow's prior estimates, ranking Chernobyl as the most costly catastrophe in Soviet peacetime history.

> "The April 26, 1986, accident was 'the biggest socioeconomic cataclysm in (peacetime) history.'"

The study, by a Soviet nuclear-industry economist, estimates that by the year 2000 the Chernobyl accident may cost the country 170 billion to 215 billion rubles in lost electricity production, contaminated farmland and other economic consequences. Moscow's previous estimate, which counted only the immediate cleanup costs, was 10 billion rubles.

Because the ruble isn't freely convertible, the new estimate can't be expressed accurately in Western currencies. At the official exchange rate in Moscow, it amounts to $283 billion to $358 billion. In any currency, the sum far exceeds cost-estimates for such previous Soviet disasters as the 1988 Armenian earthquake. The April 26, 1986, accident was "the biggest socioeconomic cataclysm in (peacetime) history," the study says, adding that Chernobyl also contributed to the country's worsening economic problems.

The Costs of Contamination

The study supports Western speculation that Moscow initially underestimated Chernobyl's cost. But its scheduled publication in Soviet news media will contribute to a mounting internal debate over the accident's cleanup costs. Local government officials near the Ukrainian reactor are pressing Moscow to provide 35 billion rubles in projected cleanup expenses. . . .

The report was commissioned by a participant in this debate, and is thus a rare example of a Soviet special-interest group learning such Western lobbying tech-

Chernobyl's consequences ramified beyond threats to health to engulf the Soviet economy. (AP Images.)

niques as commissioning research. The study's sponsor was the Chernobyl Union, an organization of accident survivors pressing Moscow for more aid. The economist who performed the study is Yuri Koryakin, chief economist of the Research and Development Institute of Power Engineering, a Soviet government institute that designed the Chernobyl reactor. In an interview, Mr. Koryakin said he agreed to conduct the study in the interests of promoting wider public debate about the Chernobyl accident.

Mr. Koryakin's findings will likely be contested by some Soviet officials. But to minimize official criticism, he said, his study used only information culled from previous Soviet publications—and avoided use of any of his institute's official, nonpublic documents. He said, however, that he believes his study is the first anywhere in the Soviet government to attempt to add together all the direct and indirect accident costs.

Cleanup and study of the Chernobyl accident has become a major, permanent segment of Soviet industry. The accident, caused when operators lost control of a reactor, spewed radiation for days over the surrounding Ukrainian, Byelorussian and Russian countryside. It forced the permanent evacuation of thousands, and contaminated about 31,000 square kilometers (12,400 square miles) of farmland and forests with long-lived radioactive cesium, strontium and other elements.

> The total bill [to clean up Chernobyl] suggests that the Soviet Union may have been better off if it had never begun building nuclear reactors in the first place.

By Mr. Koryakin's estimates, the cost of losing agricultural production on the contaminated land is among the single biggest costs of Chernobyl to the Soviet economy. From 1986 to 2000, the lost land value totals 57.5 billion to 94.5 billion rubles. A few years ago, Soviet scientists were blithely forecasting a quick return to agriculture by, for instance, using special breeds of cattle and switching them to imported, non-radioactive feed a few weeks before slaughter. But lately such optimistic talk has died out, leading some specialists to consider the contaminated land a total loss for at least two generations.

Costs of Lost Power Generation

The second-biggest economic consequence of Chernobyl, Mr. Koryakin's study says, is lost electricity production—valued at about 66.8 billion rubles through 2000. Following the accident, Soviet public opinion turned sharply against nuclear power, and Soviet authorities were forced to halt or cancel plans for 32 nuclear-power reactors.

In some areas of the Soviet Union, the nuclear cutbacks have worsened power shortages. For instance, closure of two reactors in Armenia cost the Transcaucasus region 15% of its power supply, leading to restrictions in local electricity consumption. Also, post-accident safety projects at many of the country's other reactors will raise their average electricity costs by 0.08 kopecks [one-hundredth of a ruble] a kilowatt-hour, or 9%, the study says.

Gradually decontaminating the countryside, evacuating people and completing other cleanup tasks may cost 35 billion to 45 billion rubles through 2000, the study says. Other costs include 3.9 billion to 5.1 billion rubles to install new safety equipment at Soviet reactors, and the loss of five billion rubles in capital invested in reactors closed after Chernobyl.

The total bill suggests that the Soviet Union may have been better off if it had never begun building nuclear reactors in the first place. Since the Soviets opened their first power reactor in 1954, Mr. Koryakin estimates, the net economic contribution of the Soviet nuclear industry has been 10 billion to 50 billion rubles. The sum is a measure of how much money the country saved by using cheaper, nuclear-generated electricity than more-costly coal-burning plants. The Chernobyl accident costs exceed that sum by several times.

CHAPTER 2

Controversies Surrounding the Chernobyl Disaster

Initial Reports Show the Soviet Response to Chernobyl Was Successful

Richard Wilson

Richard Wilson has authored or coauthored nearly a thousand academic articles, papers, and reports. The coauthor of *Risk Benefit Analysis*, Wilson is a recognized expert in risk analysis and management, especially pertaining to nuclear energy. Wilson visited Chernobyl in 1987, accompanied by a television crew; the visit was ultimately documented in the 1988 public television program "Back to Chernobyl."

In the following viewpoint, Wilson offers a detailed discussion of the Soviet response to the Chernobyl disaster, a response he found to be well-tempered, responsible, and largely effective. Modern readers will note that some of Wilson's assessments were overly optimistic. For example, while Wilson suggests that the Exclusion Zone and Pripyat might be resettled by 1989 or

Photo on previous page: Decades after the disaster, officials remain protective and on guard at the Chernobyl Nuclear Power Plant. (Sergei Supinsky/AFP/Getty Images.)

SOURCE. Richard Wilson, "A Visit to Chernobyl," *Science*, vol. 236, June 26, 1987, pp. 1636–1640. Copyright © 1987 by AAAS. Reproduced by permission of the author.

1990, both remain abandoned and unsafe for habitation twenty years after those suggested dates.

The first attempt to control the [Chernobyl] reactor after the accident was made by local personnel before the Moscow experts . . . arrived. Their attempt to flood the damaged reactor failed because water passed through passages between the different reactors, threatening the integrity of the adjacent units (this is a small but important design flaw). Later that day, it was realized that the graphite in the reactor was burning, and radioactivity releases were increasing. Then, on 27 April [1986] and succeeding days, 5000 metric tons of material w[ere] dropped by helicopter. This smothered the fire, but the heat of the radioactivity still kept the core hot and continued to evaporate fission products. Not until liquid nitrogen was introduced into passages below the core . . . did the core cool and the releases stop.

> "I believe that the Soviets have been remarkably successful."

By 6 May [1986] the danger was over, but the Soviets faced several huge tasks: to clean up the rest of the power station so that it could operate again; to retrain or replace the staff so the operation would be safe; to decontaminate the countryside so Soviet citizens could return to their homes; and to make enough changes in the design and operation of the RBMK reactors so they can be operated without undue risk to the Soviet people. The purpose of my visit to the power plant, and my questions of the Soviet scientists, was to see how well these tasks have been accomplished. I believe that the Soviets have been remarkably successful.

The first step was to enclose the damaged unit 4 in a sarcophagus to prevent any further release. This was finished in October [1986]. Massive new foundations were built by burrowing below the reactor, and heat exchangers were installed to allow the decay heat to be removed. Almost no radioactivity now escapes: 10 [microcuries = ten millionths of a curie, a measurement of radioactive decay] per day of ruthenium, down from 1000 [curies] per day in October, and the 100 million curies in early May. After unit 4 was enclosed, decontamination of the other units could be effective. Units 1 and 2 were restarted in October and November, respectively, and when I visited on 23 February 1987, both were in full operation, producing 2000 MW [megawatts] of electricity. Unit 3 was being decontaminated and expected to operate again no later than July; no work was being done on units 5 and 6, which were under construction at the time of the accident. I was told that construction on unit 5 was expected to start again soon, with operation planned for the end of 1989, but a more recent press report says that this has either been indefinitely delayed or cancelled. [The plant was decommissioned in 2000; neither reactor 5 nor 6 were ever completed.] The rapidity of the restart of the contaminated units 1 and 2 may be contrasted with the 6-year delay in restarting the undamaged and uncontaminated Three Mile Island unit 1. [On March 28, 1979, the Three Mile Island Nuclear Generating Station in Pennsylvania experienced a partial core meltdown.]

> The decontamination of the area around Chernobyl has proceeded better than the Soviets expected.

Decontamination of the Environment

The principal long-term problem caused by the nuclear reactor accidents is the contamination of the environment with radioactive cesium-137. Cesium is so volatile that a large amount escaped from the reactor. It has a radioactive half-life of 30 years [i.e., reducing itself by half every 30 years]. One unanticipated problem with reclamation during the hot days of summer was the blowing of the radioactive dust from a contaminated area to an uncontaminated one. Disturbing the soil by plowing may therefore be a bad idea. Nonetheless, the decontamination of the area around Chernobyl has proceeded better than the Soviets expected.

As I was driven to Chernobyl from Kiev in February 1987, radiation was not evident until we reached the outskirts of the district center of Chernobyl, where I measured 0.05 mR/Hour [milliroentgen per hour; a roentgen is a measure of radiation levels] down from 1 mR/hour on 29 May 1986. I measured 0.4 mR/hour near the village of Lelev (down from 10 mR/hour on 29 May) with a high spot of 0.7 mR/hour just north of the village, and 0.4 mR/hour in the power station parking lot just to the east of the turbine hall. The road from Kiev has been damaged by trucks, but it has not been scraped or resurfaced—only washed with chemicals. Also, until we were within 1 km [= .62 miles] of the plant, there was a little sign of scraping or ploughing the terrain on the side of the road. Inside the plant, I measured much lower levels of radiation—typically 0.06 mR/hour or less—in offices, the turbine room, and the control room. This amount leads to a modest dose for a worker of 0.1 Rem ["roentgen equivalent in man"] in a year, compared to a maximum dose of 5 Rem allowed for a radiation worker.

From the north side of the plant the road runs west to a junction within the Chernobyl-Pripyat road by the railroad bridge just south of Pripyat. This area was under the first radioactive plume. I was not taken along this road; the reason given was that snow was not yet cleared; however, I was told that the road surface has been scraped both there and in the town of Pripyat, and that the topsoil has been removed and replaced by clean soil on either side of the road. The apartment houses in Pripyat and elsewhere are quite clean; very little radioactivity got inside, but radioactivity remains on the tar roofs.

Since Chernobyl had −8°C [17.6°F] weather during my visit, the workers were waiting until spring to remove the contaminated tar.

Radioactive Contamination Decreased Quickly

In August 1986 Professor [Oleg] Pavlowski [of the Soviet Institute of Medical Physics] made cautiously pessimistic estimates of the external radiation doses and the way that they would fall with time. The doses are falling faster than he then estimated, presumably because the cesium-137 is being absorbed into the soil. The integrated dose estimates for a person at a fixed location are therefore smaller than those he previously estimated by factors of 1.5 to 2.0.

> People can now work in almost all of the houses, even those in Pripyat, and not receive a dose higher than that in the power station, which is lower than that permitted for radiation workers.

The Dnieper River is a source of drinking water for Kiev and for communities along its 200 miles southward to the Black Sea. Its purity was a source of concern since the day of the accident. Dr. [Lev] Khitrov [of the Soviet Vernatsky Institute of Geophysics and Analytical Chemistry] who went with me to Chernobyl, took charge of measuring the radioactivity in early May 1986, and showed me his data. He and his associates installed a detector in the Pripyat River 8 km [5 miles] downstream of the power plant. On 2 May, the level of radioactivity in the Dnieper River was 7×10^{-8} [curies per liter] and 2×10^{-7} [curies]/liter on its tributary, the Pripyat River. By 14 to 20 May 1986 the levels at the Kiev hydro station on the Dnieper had fallen to 1 to 5×10^{-9} [curies]/liter, about the drinking water standard. As of February 1987, they were between 1 and 2×10^{-11} [curies]/liter in the Pripyat River, 1/400 of the drinking water standard. This is about the natural level of radioactivity of potassium-40 in the oceans. Dr. Khitrov believes that most of the cesium-137 remains in the sediment. As the thaw brings the spring runoff to the river, he will check again to determine whether turbulence increases the activity. The radioactivity is further diluted in the reservoir for Kiev and is insignificant. During the summer of 1986, artesian wells were dug to provide a supply for Kiev, but they were not necessary and have not been used.

Resettlement of the Exclusion Zone

People can now work in almost all of the houses, even those in Pripyat, and not receive a dose higher than that in the power station, which is lower than that permitted for radiation workers. After the roofs are cleaned in the spring, it is expected that people can return and spend longer periods of time living in the houses without exceeding the 0.5 Rem tolerance for the general public. Many of the evacuees have better housing than before but most,

> Accidents . . . have many contributory causes. The RBMK reactor at Chernobyl has one atrocious design feature, and . . . there were management and operator errors.

and in particular the elderly, want to go "home" as soon as possible. However, the Ukrainian authorities and their Soviet advisers are being cautious about resettlement. Fourteen villages in Belorussia [Belarus] have already been resettled, and the evacuation zone of 35 km [22 miles] is expected to shrink soon to 20 km [12.4 miles] in the south to the River Ouge, just south of the town of Chernobyl.

Further decisions about resettlement have not yet been made. Many of the families live on small farms. It would not be possible to stop them from growing food, and it is important that they be able to eat what they grow. At the Vienna meeting, Academician [Leonid] Ilyin [the advisor who oversaw the evacuation following the accident] and Professor Pavlowski presented a delib-

People who have returned to the Exclusion Zone subsist off its lands and waters. (Daniel Berehulak/Getty Images.)

erately pessimistic figure of 210 million person-Rem for the integrated internal lifetime dose to the people of Belorussia and the Ukraine. Western specialists thought that this estimate was at least ten times too large, based on measurements of intake of cesium from bomb tests. Although he recognizes this, Professor Pavlowski prefers to wait until measurements of the new agricultural growth in spring 1987 are made before making any recommendations.

Distinction must be made between small, peasant farming . . . and the large collective farms. Some restrictions on the types of crops that farmers are allowed to plant may be necessary, and the enforcement of these restrictions may only be possible on collective farms. . . .

International Cooperation for Atomic Safety

Accidents in the modern technological age have many contributory causes. The RBMK reactor at Chernobyl has one atrocious design feature, and several that made it inferior to Western designs; there were management and operator errors. We obviously want to avoid all of these problems in the future and minimize their interactions.

The Soviets also want to collaborate with the West on safer designs. It is worth noting that Academician Andrei Sakharov, at the "Forum on a Nuclear Free World," held in Moscow, 14 to 16 February [1987], made a plea to those in the West who are opposing nuclear power stations. He noted, as he has before, that the world will need nuclear energy and called upon the "antinukes" to spend their energies on making reactors safer instead of opposing them.

General Secretary [of the Soviet Communist Party] Mikhail Gorbachev has called for greater international cooperation on reactor safety and has proposed that this be done through the International Atomic Energy Agency. However, safety demands openness and cooperation in personal as well as institutional ways.

It is clearly in the interest of the Soviet Union that U.S. reactors are run safely. The friendliness, openness, and unfailing courtesy that I met on my visit suggest to me that we may be able to work together toward this goal. If we cannot, I do not see how we can work together on issues where our self-interest is less evident, and the future of the world will be bleak.

Radiation Exposure and Negative Health Outcomes Were Underreported and Underestimated

Glenn Alan Cheney

Glenn Alan Cheney has authored more than twenty books on a diverse range of topics, including several on atomic weapons, nuclear testing, nuclear proliferation, and the environment. Cheney was in the Soviet Union when it dissolved in 1991, and spent six weeks traveling around Chernobyl and Kiev, the capital of the now independent nation of Ukraine, just seventy miles south of the reactor.

The following viewpoint is drawn from the resulting book, *Journey to Chernobyl: Encounters in a Radioactive Zone*. In this viewpoint, Cheney demonstrates that, owing to many lay-

---

SOURCE. Glenn Alan Cheney, *Journey to Chernobyl: Encounters in a Radioactive Zone*. Chicago, IL: Academy Chicago Publishers, 1995. Copyright © 1995 Glenn Alan Cheney. Reproduced by permission of Academy Chicago Publishers.

ers of bureaucracy and self-interested manipulation of data, it is impossible to say how severe the radiation exposure was that resulted from the Chernobyl accident, how many people were affected, and if ongoing birth defects and diseases that are increasingly difficult to diagnose and treat are the result of radioactive contamination from the Chernobyl explosion.

[M]y driver] Volodya . . . takes me . . . to a nearby address and up the rattletrap elevator to the cramped, clean apartment of a chemist named Alec who is on two committees that are measuring radioactivity all over Ukraine, figuring out which towns go in which zones. He tells us that Zone One, which is designated as being any place having more radiation than Zone Two, was supposedly evacuated in 1986. . . .

Alec says that people are still being moved out of Zone Two [in 1991], and those in Zone Three have the right to be relocated. People in Zone Four have certain economic privileges. No agricultural production is allowed in Zones Two and Three: food is being brought in to people still living there.

But of course, Alec says, things don't work out that way. People still live in all the zones, including the Prohibited Zone within thirty kilometers of the Chernobyl plant. In the absence of anything else to eat, crops are grown and consumed in all zones. Wood cook-fires send more radionuclides [radioactive substances] into the air. The Ukrainian government says that Kiev is not contaminated. Alec says that all of Kiev qualifies as Zone Four. Some parts of Kiev even qualify as Zone Three.

The trouble is, people living in Zone Four are entitled to certain ben-

> If Kiev is in Zone Four, the government of Ukraine, already all but broke, will lose a major source of revenue. [Therefore,] Kiev is not in Zone Four. It's as clean as can be. It's just a matter of ignoring numbers.

efits, including exemption from income taxation. If Kiev is in Zone Four, the government of Ukraine, already all but broke, will lose a major source of revenue.

Conclusion: Kiev is not in Zone Four. It's as clean as can be. It's just a matter of ignoring numbers.

Alec explains how bathrooms pick up more radiation because radioactive water from the Dnieper [River] runs through the pipes, which pick it up and hold it. He shows me a little dosimeter. For 110 rubles I could buy one in any store, he says. Then I'll always know for sure. We turn it on. It says 0.13 milliroentgens per hour. 0.10 would be normal. Outdoors, he says, it would be 0.14. This is called background radiation. It's always there.

[My translator] Ljudmula and I go to a press conference back at the International Conference. No good news there. Genetic abnormalities are up 1.8 times. Cancer is way up, especially in children. But most of what I hear is the hogwash of people with political aspira-

Clashing agendas and layers of bureaucracy have made it difficult to determine how many people the Chernobyl accident affected—and in what ways. (Chuck Nacke/ Time Life Pictures/Getty Images.)

tions. . . . We leave to go see a city deputy named Skripka.

Skripka's a former plant physiologist. He hasn't got any good news either. He's got all kinds of data and it looks organized, comprehensive, and accurate. I trust it because it's coming from a former plant physiologist who is wearing a suit and tie that are up to Western snuff. His data is on computer print-outs.

Widespread Exposure to Radiation

Skripka's theory is that there are more victims of Chernobyl than is officially known. Some 30,000 liquidators [workers who cleaned up the disaster site in the immediate aftermath of the accident] and evacuees have registered as victims, but Skripka believes there are 20,000 more who haven't bothered. But even those numbers are low, he says. Everyone in Kiev—2.6 million people—is a victim because radiation is much higher than officially acknowledged. His data falls in line with that of Alec the chemist. Though Skripka cannot verify it, some scientists he knows went to the Soviet Union's nuclear testing ground and took radiation readings at ground zero. The readings were lower there than at any place in Kiev.

By Skripka's estimate, in the days following the accident, everyone in Kiev received from three to five rem from internal radiation. (Five rem is the maximum annual dose allowed nuclear workers in the United States.) The most dangerous internal doses are alpha and beta particles emitted from radionuclides. Alpha radiation is relatively harmless as long as the source has not penetrated your corporeal fortress [body]. They can be stopped by a sheet of paper or human skin. Beta particles can barely penetrate skin. But if the radionuclides that emit these particles are inhaled or swallowed, the body may accept some of them as nutrients. Strontium-90, for example, behaves a lot like calcium. It has the same number of valence electrons in its outer shell. Bones readily latch on to it. The strontium makes itself at home and begins radiating the local marrow.

Similarly, iodine-131 is quite like regular iodine, so it tends to accumulate in the thyroid. (The purpose of iodine pills as a safeguard against radiation is to fill the thyroid so the radioactive iodine just passes out of the body as an unneeded nutrient.) Cesium is versatile enough to find many homes in the human organism.

> Thirty percent of children can't receive a vaccination, because they come down with the disease the vaccination was supposed to prevent.

Once lodged in the body, these radionuclides keep emitting radiation, attacking the thyroid, the marrow, the blood that happens to pass by. It might give you thyroid cancer, leukemia, or any of various blood diseases. A barely visible speck of plutonium in your lung is enough to give you lung cancer.

Kiev was also bombarded by gamma radiation. It zaps right through the human body, doing some damage on the way but not lingering to continue the attack. Today, scientists cannot determine how many rem of gamma waves people suffered [after the accident].

Skripka gained access to some KGB [Soviet intelligence] files and found that the Soviet government knew a lot more than it let on. Children under the age of one had an average dose of .5 rem to their thyroids—half the current annual dose allowed to hit non-nuclear workers in the United States. Pregnant women and their unborn were known to have equal radiation levels in their blood. Breast milk was contaminated. . . .

A special well dug in the Prohibited Zone brings water up from thirty meters. Lately it's been showing radiation levels of ten picocuries per liter. [A picocurie is one-trillionth curie.] If it were a byproduct in a nuclear laboratory, you'd have to take special measures to dispose of it. Dropping it into a well would not be appropriate.

The Dnieper River, which runs through the center of Kiev, once had similar levels of strontium, but it has dropped to one picocurie—acceptable though still above the ideal of zero.

Degraded Immune Systems

So it's no wonder blood donor data shows that eighty percent of donors have abnormal levels of such things as white and red blood cells and immune proteins. It explains why thirty percent of children can't receive a vaccination, because they come down with the disease the vaccination was supposed to prevent.

Skripka has data on increases in health problems. Among official adult victims, the death rate has increased 400 percent since 1987. Death by cancer is up 300 percent. Breast cancer is up twenty-six percent. General disease, up 500 percent. Problems in thyroids and other glands, up 400 percent. Respiratory disease, excluding cancer and tuberculosis, up 2,000 percent. Pneumonia, up 220 percent in adults, 260 percent in children. Allergy problems, up forty-one percent in adults, eighty percent in children. Incidence of brain cancer, up 350 percent from 1988 to 1991. Genetic aberration, ten to thirteen times higher in contaminated areas.

> It's information like this that makes heads roll.

This information flies in the face of the conclusion of the United Nations International Atomic Energy Agency (IAEA). The IAEA made a supposedly comprehensive and unbiased assessment of the aftereffects of Chernobyl to see if people who have not been evacuated are suffering consequences of radiation. (They did not examine liquidators or evacuees.) The IAEA conclusion: no problem. There is no illness, no cancer, no increase in birth defects. Even people living in the most contaminated areas, the areas marked blood red on contamination maps, are suffering no more than they did under [Soviet leaders

> Some of the doctors on the teams refused to finish the job because they thought it wasn't being done scientifically or independently.

Joseph] Stalin, [Nikita] Khrushchev and [Leonid] Brezhnev.

Skripka says what the UN has done is certify the safety of nuclear war. If their report is true, he says, if fifty tons of nuclear fuel can be thrown into the atmosphere without harming anyone, why don't we dispose of nuclear waste the same way—just stack it on a pile of dynamite and blow it up?

Skripka announced a press conference where he planned to disseminate his information, which was probably the most complete and accurate available anywhere. Unfortunately, no one showed up. He suspects they were afraid to. They depend on the government for their paper and other supplies. The government of Kiev might like to have this information made public, but the government of Ukraine would not. He says he has many enemies on his committee. They don't like this information. They're bureaucrats, and it's information like this that makes heads roll. . . .

Shoddy Verification of Soviet Data

[A video screened at the local Greenpeace office] is produced by the UN's International Atomic Energy Agency (IAEA), touting its comprehensive scientific investigations in contaminated areas. It shows the radiologists setting up equipment, taking soil samples, examining leaves, poking around homes. It shows doctors feeling kids' throats, measuring people for this and that. They formed three teams: the historical team was to figure out what happened, minute by minute; the radiation team was to assess contamination of soil, water, food, houses, etc.; the medical team would measure radiation and its effects on people. The team's declared purpose was mainly to examine the validity of the official Soviet methodology and verify its findings through field sampling.

AVERAGE ACCUMULATED RADIATION DOSES TO AFFECTED POPULATIONS FROM CHERNOBYL FALLOUT		
Population Category	Number of People	Average Dose in Millisievert (mSv)
Liquidators (1986–1989)	600,000	~100
Evacuees from highly-contaminated zone (1986)	116,000	33
Residents of "strict-control" zones (1986–2005)	270,000	>50
Residents of other "contaminated" areas (1986–2005)	5,000,000	10–20

Taken from: IAEA Chernobyl Forum 2003–2005, Chernobyl's Legacy: Health, Environmental and Socio-Economic Impacts and Recommendations to the Governments of Belarus, the Russian Federation and Ukraine, April 2006, www.iaea.org/Publications/Booklets/Chernobyl/chernobyl.pdf.

So I'm watching and taking notes when a girl named Olga turns from her computer and asks me what I think about what I'm seeing. I say it looks like they did a pretty thorough job. She says it wasn't like that.

I hit the pause button.

Olga was part of the UN team, a translator. She says the sampling was pretty scanty and that the team went only into areas suggested by the Soviets. Their sampling verified the Soviet data, but she thinks the Soviets were careful about which data they revealed. Most of the investigation was just a matter of looking over the masses of information and deciding that it somehow looked right. Some of the doctors on the teams refused to finish the job because they thought it wasn't being done scientifically or independently.

Not only did the IAEA find *no aftereffects from the accident*, but it also said that criteria for evacuation—the radiation levels that establish Zones One to Four—are too restrictive. Moving people out of even the most highly

> *Everything* in their bodies is breaking down and there is no single explanation for it.

contaminated areas would do them little good; wherever they went to live they would pick up almost as much radiation from normal background sources like the sun and radon gas.

Olga has seen evidence to the contrary. Her mother is a doctor in a trauma center. From 1990 through 1992 more and more liquidators have been coming in with mysterious complaints. They have terrible headaches, sudden changes in blood pressure, inexplicable fevers. Traditional treatments not only don't work but even produce contrary reactions: raising blood pressure instead of lowering it, or worsening the headaches. There is no statistical data base from which to draw conclusions, but any doctor can confirm that something different, something *odd*, is happening.

The trouble is, these vague but very real and even deadly complaints could just as easily result from good old-fashioned chemical pollution—the lead in the milk, the pesticides on the crops, the fertilizers in the water, the hydrocarbons in the air. Just about everybody smokes, which means any given room holds a haze the color of tar vapor; even kids must suck in a risky dose. Worsening the problem, virtually no one is eating a balanced diet. Milk is all but impossible to find and too suspect to drink even if you could find it. So everybody lacks calcium, a deficiency which happens to affect the immune system. When a kid contracts measles from a measles vaccine, is it because of radiation or the lack of calcium caused by a *fear* of radiation in milk? I guess the question's moot to the kid who has measles for three months. . . .

Systemic Collapse

I get some good information at the children's hospital. A calm, exhausted doctor named Olga tells me that Ukraine, as a whole, is in terrible health. She does not claim any significant increases in cancer, leukemia or birth defects. The problem is in the general state of health. Everybody, especially children, has a *generally* poor state of health. *Everything* in their bodies is breaking down and there is no single explanation for it. This problem has certainly worsened since Chernobyl, and especially over the last couple of years. But Chernobyl is not the only culprit. The pollution and malnutrition combine to weaken and attack the body. Just as important, perhaps, is the stress of knowing that all this is happening to everyone, plus the stress of unemployment or chronic underemployment, plus not knowing if there will be any food in town, let alone in the cupboard, by the end of the winter, let alone by the next harvest, plus the inevitable family problems produced by hunger, illness, poverty, alcoholism and living in close quarters, plus they really don't even know what kind of a country they live in or how to replace the ruins of the centrally planned economy, plus several of the other former Soviet states are breaking out in civil war, which could happen in Ukraine, which is artificially attached to Crimea, which doesn't like being Ukrainian. It's all enough to make anybody sick.

> This isn't an illness; it's a syndrome. It's an immune deficiency, and it's acquired from the environment.

The combination produces what Olga calls the synergy effect. The sum of the ills is greater than the combined normal prognoses. In fact, the sum of the ills is an illness nobody's ever seen before. It varies from individual to individual. It's as if each person had a new and unique disease. You can't tell which is deadly, which will cure itself. Measles isn't just measles anymore. Treatments don't yield normal results. Textbooks no longer apply. The medical progress of the twentieth century doesn't count for much. They're starting from scratch.

What they're dealing with is a syndrome resulting

from a massive attack on the body's immune system. The body, starved for nutrients, is glad to latch onto whatever elements come onboard, even if it's cesium, strontium or plutonium. The isotopes make themselves right at home, radiating the immediately surrounding areas and all the blood that passes by.

"Chernobyl AIDS"

This isn't an illness; it's a syndrome. It's an immune deficiency, and it's acquired from the environment. Put it all together and it spells AIDS. HIV doesn't necessarily enter into it (though often enough it does), so people refer to it as Chernobyl AIDS. Unlike HIV, it isn't contagious, but like HIV, it has no cure.

The real problem, properly defined, isn't the suppressed immune system but the unpredictable responses to treatments. The diseases are unique and the treatments are unknown.

Olga thinks the solution lies not just in building another hospital or institute, but rather in recognizing the problem and developing a new medical specialty. Of course no such action is being considered in Ukraine or anywhere else in the world.

Another doctor, dark and serious, tells me that this new medical information is not completely new to the world. A considerable body of data exists in the Moscow Scientific Institute, but it is classified, so no one has access to it. The data comes from victims of a nuclear accident at Chelyabinsk and also people subjected to nearby atomic tests. This doctor saw secret papers referring to this data and had already deduced its existence when Moscow sent investigators after the Chernobyl catastrophe. From the questions they asked, it was clear they had encountered similar problems in the past. They already knew it would take Ukrainian doctors several years to figure out through trial and error with thousands of human guinea pigs.

Doctors call this "catastrophe medicine"—the necessary use of patients for experimentation, the direct application of theory to practice.

What Olga and her colleagues have done at this particular hospital is develop a computer program that analyzes *all* of a patient's functions to produce a single holistic treatment for a given individual's multifarious ailments. It works well, or would if they had the medicines the treatments require. But this is a hospital without medicines. They don't even have a ribbon for the computer printer. They show me a print-out. It's too faint to read in a room that's down to its last light bulb.

Olga lets me walk around to take pictures of half-dead kids who are conceivably radiation victims. One is a very small girl with acute immunodeficiency which has led to kidney failure. A fat little baby suffers multiple genetic abnormalities, including Down's Syndrome and lack of anus. Another is a boy just withering away for reasons unknown. Another boy was doing fine until his father got drunk and smashed up his car with his son in the passenger seat. Now the child is in a coma. A psychic is with him, waving her hands over him as if caressing an invisible essence outside his body. A doctor says the boy showed a little response, a movement of a leg. The doctor doesn't look optimistic. He says the psychic is a last resort.

Radiation Exposure from the Chernobyl Disaster Was Not as Severe as Expected

International Atomic Energy Agency

The following viewpoint is drawn from a report compiled by the Chernobyl Forum for the twentieth anniversary of the Chernobyl disaster. The Chernobyl Forum comprises nine United Nations agencies (the International Atomic Energy Agency, the Food and Agriculture Organization, the United Nations Office for the Coordination of Humanitarian Affairs, the United Nations Development Programme, the United Nations Environment Programme, the United Nations Scientific Committee on the Effects of Atomic Radiation, the World Health Organization, and the World Bank), and the governments of Ukraine, Russia, and Belarus. The report provides a detailed analysis of the immediate and lasting health, environmental, and socio-economic dam-

SOURCE. International Atomic Energy Agency Chernobyl Forum: 2003–2005, *Chernobyl's Legacy, The Chernobyl Forum: 2003–2005.* Vienna, Austria: International Atomic Energy Agency, IAEA, 2006. Reproduced by permission.

ages caused by the Chernobyl meltdown, as well as a detailed set of recommendations to the most-affected nations (Belarus, Ukraine, and Russia). The report ultimately concludes that the greatest lingering threat caused by the Chernobyl accident is not exposure to radiation, but the profound long-term mental health impact of exaggerated fears about the impact of radioactive exposure.

The number of deaths attributable to the Chernobyl accident has been of paramount interest to the general public, scientists, the mass media, and politicians. Claims have been made that tens or even hundreds of thousands of persons have died as a result of the accident. These claims are highly exaggerated. Confusion about the impact of Chernobyl on mortality has arisen owing to the fact that, in the years since 1986, thousands of emergency and recovery operation workers as well as people who lived in 'contaminated' territories have died of diverse natural causes that are not attributable to radiation. However, widespread expectations of ill health and a tendency to attribute all health problems to exposure to radiation have led local residents to assume that Chernobyl-related fatalities were much higher.

Acute Radiation Syndrome Mortality

The number of deaths due to acute radiation syndrome (ARS) during the first year following the accident is well documented. According to UNSCEAR [United Nations Scientific Committee on the Effects of Atomic Radiation] (2000), ARS was diagnosed in 134 emergency workers. In many cases the ARS was complicated by extensive beta radiation skin burns and sepsis [body-wide infection]. Among these workers, 28 persons died in 1986 due to ARS. Two more persons had died at Unit 4 from injuries unrelated to radiation, and one additional death was thought to have been due to a coronary thrombosis.

Nineteen more have died in 1987–2004 of various causes; however their deaths are not necessarily—and in some cases are certainly not—directly attributable to radiation exposure. Among the general population exposed to the Chernobyl radio-active fallout, however, the radiation doses were relatively low, and ARS and associated fatalities did not occur.

Cancer Mortality

It is impossible to assess reliably, with any precision, numbers of fatal cancers caused by radiation exposure due to Chernobyl accident. Further, radiation-induced cancers are at present indistinguishable from those due to other causes.

An international expert group has made projections to provide a rough estimate of the possible health impacts of the accident and to help plan the future allocation of public health resources. These predictions were based on the experience of other populations exposed to radiation that have been studied for many decades, such as the survivors of the atomic bombing in Hiroshima and Nagasaki. However, the applicability of risk estimates derived from other populations with different genetic, life-style and environmental backgrounds, as well as having been exposed to much higher radiation dose rates, is unclear. Moreover small differences in the assumptions about the risks from exposure to low level radiation doses can lead to large differences in the predictions of the increased cancer burden, and predictions should therefore be treated with great caution, especially when the additional doses above natural background radiation are small.

The international expert group predicts that among the 600,000 persons receiving more significant exposures (liquidators [people who cleaned up after the accident] working 1986–1987, evacuees, and residents of the most 'contaminated' areas), the possible increase in cancer mortality due to this radiation exposure might be up to a few per cent. This might eventually represent up to four thousand fatal cancers in addition to the approximately 100,000 fatal cancers to be expected due to all other causes in this population. Among the 5 million persons residing in other 'contaminated' areas, the doses are much lower and any projected increases are more speculative, but are expected to make a difference of less than one per cent in cancer mortality.

> "Epidemiological studies of residents of contaminated areas in Belarus, Russia and Ukraine have not provided clear and convincing evidence for a radiation-induced increase in general population mortality."

Such increases would be very difficult to detect with available epidemiological tools, given the normal variation in cancer mortality rates. So far, epidemiological studies of residents of contaminated areas in Belarus, Russia and Ukraine have not provided clear and convincing evidence for a radiation-induced increase in general population mortality, and in particular, for fatalities caused by leukaemia, solid cancers (other than thyroid cancer), and non-cancer diseases.

However, among the more than 4000 thyroid cancer cases diagnosed in 1992–2002 in persons who were children or adolescents at the time of the accident, fifteen deaths related to the progression of the disease had been documented by 2002.

Some radiation-induced increases in fatal leukaemia, solid cancers and circulatory system diseases have been reported in Russian emergency and recovery operation workers. According to data from the Russian Registry, in 1991–1998, in the cohort of 61,000 Russian workers exposed to an average dose of 107 mSv [millisieverts— about forty times the exposure from background radiation], about 5% of all fatalities that occurred may have been due to radiation exposure. These findings, however, should be considered as preliminary and need confirma-

tion in better-designed studies with careful individual dose reconstruction. . . .

Thyroid Cancer in Children

One of the principal radionuclides released by the Chernobyl accident was iodine-131, which was significant for the first few months. The thyroid gland accumulates iodine from the blood stream as part of its normal metabolism. Therefore, fallout of radio-active iodines led to considerable thyroid exposure of local residents through inhalation and ingestion of foodstuffs, especially milk, containing high levels of radioiodine. The thyroid gland is one of the organs most susceptible to cancer induction by radiation. Children were found to be the most vulnerable population, and a substantial increase in thyroid cancer among those exposed as children was recorded subsequent to the accident.

From 1992 to 2002 in Belarus, Russia and Ukraine more than 4000 cases of thyroid cancer were diagnosed among those who were children and adolescents (0–18 years) at the time of the accident, the age group 0–14 years being most affected. The majority of these cases were treated, with favourable prognosis for their lives. Given the rarity of thyroid cancer in young people, the large population with high doses to the thyroid and the magnitude of the radiation-related risk estimates derived from epidemiological studies, it is most likely that a large fraction of thyroid cancers observed to date among those exposed in childhood are attributable to radiation exposure from the accident. It is expected that the increase in thyroid cancer incidence from Chernobyl will continue for many more years, although the long term magnitude of risk is difficult to quantify.

It should be noted that early mitigation measures taken by the national authorities helped substantially to minimize the health consequences of the accident. Intake of stable iodine tablets during the first 6–30 hours after

Photo on previous page: Animal specimens from the woods near Chernobyl showed genetic alteration that appeared not to affect the creatures' daily lives. (Patrick Landmann/Getty Images.)

Three Mile Island

Three Mile Island, the site of the worst civilian nuclear power program accident in the United States, is located in the Susquehanna River near Harrisburg, Pennsylvania. In the early 1970s, Metropolitan Edison built two reactors on Three Mile Island for commercial energy production. On 28 March 1979, a faulty valve allowed water coolant to escape from Metropolitan Edison's second reactor, Unit 2, during an unplanned shutdown. A cascade of human errors and technological mishaps resulted in an overheated reactor core with temperatures as high as 4,300 degrees and the accidental release of radiation into the atmosphere. Plant operators struggled to resolve the situation. Press reporters highlighted the confusion surrounding the accident, while Governor Richard L. Thornburgh of Pennsylvania and President Jimmy Carter visited the stricken plant, urging the nation to remain calm. On 30 March, state officials evacuated preg-

nant women and preschool children from the immediate area as a safety measure. On 2 April, temperatures decreased inside the Unit 2 reactor, and government officials declared the crisis over on 9 April.

A commission authorized by President Carter investigated the calamity. Government analysts calculated that, at the height of the crisis, Unit 2 was within approximately one hour of a meltdown and a significant breach of containment. The lessons learned at Three Mile Island led to improved safety protocols and equipment overhauls at commercial reactors across the country. Three Mile Island also contributed to rising public anxiety over the safety of nuclear energy.

SOURCE. *Robert M. Guth and John Wills, "Three Mile Island,"* Dictionary of American History, *edited by Stanley I. Kutler, vol. 8, 3rd ed. New York: Charles Scribner's Sons, 2003.*

the accident reduced the thyroid dose of the residents of Pripyat by a factor of 6 on average. Pripyat was the largest city nearest to the Chernobyl nuclear plant and approximately 50,000 residents were evacuated within 40 hours after the accident. More than 100,000 people were evacuated within few weeks after the accident from the most contaminated areas of Ukraine and Belarus. These actions reduced radiation exposures and reduced the radiation related health impacts of the accident.

Leukaemia, Solid Cancers, and Circulatory Diseases

A number of epidemiological studies, including atomic bombing survivors, patients treated with radiotherapy and occupationally exposed populations in medicine and the nuclear industry, have shown that ionizing radiation can cause solid cancers and leukaemia [except a chronic lymphoid leukaemia that is not thought to be caused by radiation exposure]. More recent findings also indicate an increased risk of cardiovascular diseases in populations exposed at higher doses (e.g. atomic bombing survivors, radiotherapy patients).

An increased risk of leukaemia associated with radiation exposure from Chernobyl was, therefore, expected among the populations exposed. Given the level of doses received, however, it is likely that studies of the general population will lack statistical power to identify such an increase, although for higher exposed emergency and recovery operation workers an increase may be detectable. The most recent studies suggest a two-fold increase in the incidence of non-CLL leukaemia between 1986 and 1996 in Russian emergency and recovery operation workers exposed to more than 150 mGy [milligrays—more than 100 times the amount of radiation absorbed by a patient getting an X-ray at the doctor's office] (external dose). Ongoing studies of the workers may provide additional information on the possible increased risk of leukaemia.

However, since the risk of radiation-induced leukaemia decreases

> There is . . . no convincing evidence at present that the incidence of leukaemia or cancer . . . has increased in children, those exposed in-utero, or adult residents of the 'contaminated' areas.

> Birth rates may be lower in 'contaminated' areas because of concern about having children . . . and the fact that many younger people have moved away.

several decades after exposure, its contribution to morbidity and mortality is likely to become less significant as time progresses.

There have been many post-Chernobyl studies of leukaemia and cancer morbidity in the populations of 'contaminated' areas in the three countries. Most studies, however, had methodological limitations and lacked statistical power. There is therefore no convincing evidence at present that the incidence of leukaemia or cancer (other than thyroid) has increased in children, those exposed in-utero, or adult residents of the 'contaminated' areas. It is thought, however, that for most solid cancers, the minimum latent period is likely to be much longer than that for leukaemia or thyroid cancer—of the order of 10 to 15 years or more—and it may be too early to evaluate the full radiological impact of the accident. Therefore, medical care and annual examinations of highly exposed Chernobyl workers should continue.

The absence of a demonstrated increase in cancer risk—apart from thyroid cancer—is not proof that no increase has in fact occurred. Such an increase, however, is expected to be very difficult to identify in the absence of careful large scale epidemiological studies with individual dose estimates. It should be noted that, given the large number of individuals exposed, small differences in the models used to assess risks at low doses can have marked effects on the estimates of additional cancer cases.

There appears to be some recent increase in morbidity and mortality of Russian emergency and recovery operation workers caused by circulatory system diseases. Incidence of circulatory system diseases should be interpreted with special care because of the possible indirect influence of confounding factors, such as stress and lifestyle. These findings also need confirmation in well-designed studies.

Radiation-Caused Cataracts

Examinations of eyes of children and emergency and recovery operation workers clearly show that cataracts [a clouding of the lens] may develop in association with exposure to radiation from the Chernobyl accident. The data from studies of emergency and recovery workers suggest that exposures to radiation somewhat lower than previously experienced, down to about 250 mGy, may be cataractogenic [cause cataracts].

Continued eye follow-up studies of the Chernobyl populations will allow confirmation and greater predictive capability of the risk of radiation cataract onset and, more importantly, provide the data necessary to be able to assess the likelihood of any resulting visual dysfunction.

Accident Did Not Cause Birth Defects

Because of the relatively low dose levels to which the populations of the Chernobyl-affected regions were exposed, there is no evidence or any likelihood of observing decreased fertility among males or females in the general population as a direct result of radiation exposure. These doses are also unlikely to have any major effect on the number of stillbirths, adverse pregnancy outcomes or delivery complications or the overall health of children.

Birth rates may be lower in 'contaminated' areas because of concern about having children (this issue is obscured by the very high rate of medical abortions) and the fact that many younger people have moved away. No discernable increase in hereditary effects caused by radiation is expected based on the low risk coefficients estimated by UNSCEAR (2001) or in previous reports on Chernobyl health effects. Since 2000, there has been no new evidence provided to change this conclusion.

There has been a modest but steady increase in reported congenital malformations in both 'contaminated' and 'uncontaminated' areas of Belarus since 1986. This does not appear to be radiation-related and may be the result of increased registration.

Belarus Absorbed the Brunt of Chernobyl's Radiation

Fred Weir

Fred Weir is a Canadian journalist and the coauthor of *Revolution from Above: The Demise of the Soviet System*. He resides in Moscow and focuses primarily on developments in Russia and other parts of formerly Soviet Europe.

In the following viewpoint Weir explains that although the Chernobyl reactor was located in Ukraine, roughly 70 percent of the radioactive fallout from the accident landed in neighboring Belarus. This contaminated 20 percent of the country, an area still occupied by 1.5 million Belarusians. According to the author, the Belarusian government claims to annually spend exorbitant sums on Chernobyl's consequences, all the while scolding Western countries for not coming to their aid. Meanwhile, Belarus's complicated and uncooperative bureaucracy makes it next to impossible for domestic agencies, citizens' groups,

SOURCE. Fred Weir, "Still Under Chernobyl's Shadow; Twenty Years After the Disaster, Hard-Hit Belarus Has Yet to Get Substantial Aid," *The Christian Science Monitor*, April 26, 2006, p. 1. Copyright © 2006 The Christian Science Publishing Society. Reproduced by permission.

foreign and domestic experts, and international aid agencies to coordinate their efforts.

When the Chernobyl nuclear reactor exploded 20 years ago [in 1986], pouring radiation equivalent to more than 100 Hiroshima bombs into the air, the people of this small agricultural village a few miles downwind didn't flee.

"No one warned us about the danger. We were left in the dark," says Alexander Malinovsky, a boy at the time. No effort was ever made to evacuate people from Svetilovichi, says Mr. Malinovsky, who still farms his father's small plot here, deep inside Belarus's highly contaminated "exclusion zone." And little has been done since to help them adjust, he adds.

> Over a fifth of [Belarus] is still considered heavily contaminated, with 1.5 million people living in those areas.

In the two decades since one of the world's worst environmental disasters, gobal attention—and aid—has largely focused on Ukraine, where the Chernobyl plant is located. But the plight of Belarus, where 70 percent of Chernobyl's nuclear fallout descended, is less well known. Over a fifth of the country is still considered heavily contaminated, with 1.5 million people living in those areas. Some, like the Malinovskys, inhabit dangerous hot spots that authorities have sealed off with barbed-wire—which are reachable only by negotiating special police checkpoints.

Dozens of shuttered and crumbling houses along Svetilovichi's main street suggest that many people have left town. But others, like Mr. Malinovsky and his family, say they have nowhere else to go.

"This is the land of my ancestors and I'll stay, whether it's good or bad," insists Malinovsky, who ekes out a living by hiring out his horse to plow fields and haul goods. His wife, Gertruda, earns about $100 per month as a milk-maid at a local collective farm.

Obstacles to Receiving Foreign Aid

Many people here fault President Alexander Lukashenko for the lack of international attention to Belarus's crushing nuclear legacy. Unlike democratic and relatively open Ukraine, Belarus has had trouble securing international aid.

"Lukashenko has effectively put an end to foreign aid by putting too many bureaucratic controls on it," says Vassily Yakovenko, chairman of the Chernobyl Social-Ecological Union, a grass-roots group based in the capital, Minsk. "He doesn't want foreigners here, so he keeps them out."

The authoritarian leader, who has ruled the country since 1994, has deflected the blame onto Western countries.

"Belarus didn't build Chernobyl, didn't exploit it, and didn't explode it," Mr. Lukashenko told journalists fol-

Many Belarussians blame their authoritarian president, Alexander Lukashenko, for preventing post-Chernobyl aid from other nations. (Viktor Drachev/AFP/Getty Images.)

lowing his [2006] reelection, in polls that international observers deemed fraudulent. "But we were the hardest hit. . . . Could Belarus have coped with this on its own? Instead of spending $100 billion on war, the United States might have helped us. But they don't want to."

In late March [2006], the US and the European Union slapped sanctions on Belarus, citing Lukashenko's crackdown on the political opposition. Opposition leader Alexander Milinkevich, who has visited several Western countries since his defeat, said that officials he's met on trips abroad have expressed concern about Chernobyl's consequences.

> 'The attitude of Western organizations toward Belarus creates obstacles to cooperation.'

"Democratic countries have a sufficient ability to help—they are interested in helping us," Mr. Milinkevich said at an opposition-organized conference in Gomel, the Belarussian city nearest to Chernobyl. "But it is difficult to work with us. Going through all the departments is torture."

Problems with International Cooperation

Observers say that bureaucratic hassle may explain delays in projects such as a $50 million World Bank initiative to bring natural-gas supplies to people in isolated villages in the exclusion zone. But deputy chair of the official State Chernobyl Committee, Valery Shevchuk, blames such delays on political maneuvering. "The attitude of Western organizations toward Belarus creates obstacles to cooperation. After all, Chernobyl is one thing; politics ought to be something different."

According to Mr. Shevchuk's committee, known as KomChernobyl, Belarus spends up to $1 billion annually dealing with the consequences of Chernobyl. "Foreign investment is very low, and we have to carry most of the burden ourselves," says Mr. Shevchuk.

Numerous nongovernmental organizations within Belarus working on Chernobyl-related issues have run into trouble. Mr. Yakovenko, of the Chernobyl Social-Ecological Union, says that growing state controls over independent activity make it difficult for his group to accomplish anything.

"We are allowed to exist formally, but it's like being in a vacuum," he says. "It's impossible to obtain any information from official sources, and there are almost no other civil-society groups that we might work with. Whatever we try to do, the government either takes [it] over or shuts [it] down."

One problem is determining the extent of the public health threat posed by radiation. A report issued by the UN's International Atomic Energy Agency (IAEA) calculated that only 50 deaths can be attributed to the accident, with perhaps 4,000 more in years to come.

The governments of both Belarus and Ukraine dispute that finding and say the death rate has been much higher among the 2 million then-Soviet citizens who were officially classed as "victims of Chernobyl."

"Our studies indicate that 34,499 people who took part in the cleanup of Chernobyl have died in the years since the catastrophe," Nikolai Omelyanets, deputy head of Ukraine's National Commission for Radiation Protection, told journalists. "All the information we sent to the IAEA has been ignored for some reason."

Other groups, including Greenpeace, have put the number closer to 100,000.

Oleg Gromyko, head of Belarus's tiny Green Party, says no serious public health studies have been done on people living in the exclusion zone around his home city of Gomel, which includes Svetilovichi. "The damage to this region has hardly been counted yet," he says. "We do not have scientific data, but all anecdotal evidence suggests it's very bad." In his own family, four of his six siblings died young—three of cancer, he says.

"We were all exposed to Chernobyl, but here I am, hale and hardy. That shows you how hard it is to get a handle on this," Mr. Gromyko explains. "Since there is no solid information, people don't know what to believe."

One group of Belarussian scientists who did try to accurately measure the effects of long-term radiation exposure in the population was broken up four years ago by the authorities and its leaders imprisoned. According to a report issued by Yakovenko's group, the group—experts with the nongovernmental Institute of Radiation Security in Minsk—had angered the government by publishing radiation figures for many Belarussian areas that were far above official estimates.

Radioactive Food

Mr. Gromyko, whose now-abandoned ancestral village of Gromyki is deep inside the exclusion zone, says much of the land that was declared too radioactive for use is being steadily turned back into farmland under orders from Lukashenko. He points out two large dairy farms inside the zone near Svetilovichy which appear to be operative.

> 'Maybe the food is radioactive, but we still need to eat.'

Mr. Shevchuk, of the official KomChernobyl, insists that all foodstuffs are carefully controlled, and that little contaminated produce makes it to market.

"What we can control, we do control," he says. "We have 2,000 laboratories all over Belarus that are constantly checking for violations. We still have problems, but we are managing."

But Yakovenko says that radiation in foodstuffs is growing as farmland is brought back into production. The authorities have gotten around this, he says, by raising the maximum level of radiation allowed in food four- or five-fold. "Statistics from this government can't be trusted," he concludes.

None of this makes much difference to Malinovsky, who grows most of the food his family consumes, and never bothers to have it checked for radiation.

"A few years ago, officials came around and told us to get rid of our cows, that drinking the milk was very dangerous," he says. "But what are we supposed to do? There's no work around here, so we have to live on our means. Maybe the food is radioactive, but we still need to eat."

Which Country Suffered the Most from Chernobyl Is Unclear

Mary Mycio

Mary Mycio is an American journalist and long-time Kiev correspondent with degrees in law and biology. She first visited Ukraine in 1989, when she secretly met with environmentalists to discuss the explosion and meltdown at the Chernobyl power plant. Her 2005 book, *Wormwood Forest: A Natural History of Chernobyl*, looks at the long-term effects the accident has had on the people, animals, and plants still living in the Zone of Alienation.

In the following viewpoint, excerpted from her book, Mycio discusses the frequently repeated but poorly sourced claim that "70 percent of the fallout from the Chernobyl accident fell on Belarus," and thus that this former Soviet republic and its people have been most hurt by the disaster. Mycio demonstrates that, in this case, attempting to calculate Chernobyl's "biggest victim" quickly descends into nebulous absurdity.

SOURCE. Mary Mycio, *The Wormwood Forest*. Washington, DC: Joseph Henry Press, 2005. Copyright © 2005 by Mary Mycio. All rights reserved. Reproduced by permission.

[P etr] Palytayev [director of the highly contaminated Polissia State Radiological and Ecological Reserve in Belarus] gave me a pamphlet printed on the occasion of the reserve's fifteenth anniversary in 2003. Displaying the reserve's logo of a triangular trefoil sign against a backdrop of conical evergreens and oak leaves, the pamphlet was an informative primer for first-time visitors and one that the Ukrainian zone—which gets many more visitors than Belarus—would do well to emulate. But after more than 18 years, the Ukrainian zone administration hadn't even put together a fact sheet, much less the colorful little booklet I held.

"The reserve contains 70 percent of the strontium-90 that fell on Belarus and 97 percent of the plutonium isotopes," I read aloud. "Exposure is as high as two milliroentgens an hour in places."

> Belarus officially maintains that 70 percent of the fallout from Chernobyl fell on its country.

I had routinely exceeded two milliroentgens during my hikes in the Red Forest [outside Chernobyl], where readings of 10 milliroentgens an hour of gamma radiation in the air are not unusual, and levels can go as high as one roentgen.

But comparing maximum exposure levels in the two zones led me to think about the various claims made on behalf of the three most affected countries—Belarus, Russia, and Ukraine—as to which country suffered most from the disaster.

Calculating Victimhood

It is often said that Belarus holds the unfortunate first place in Chernobyl victimhood. Indeed, Belarus officially maintains that 70 percent of the fallout from Chernobyl fell on its country. So do charities for Belarus's Chernobyl victims. For example, the web site of the New York–based Chernobyl Children's Project International

> Wind direction does not explain the causes of the extent of Belarus's contamination.

(CCPI), which was associated with the 2004 Oscar-winning short documentary *Chernobyl Heart*, makes that claim and says that the reason is because the prevailing winds were directed north to northwest at the time of the explosion.

But Russian and Ukrainian scientists vigorously dispute Belarus's claims. They maintain that most of the radioactive release fell on the grounds of the power station and within the borders of the 10-kilometer zone in Ukraine. Although the 70 percent figure is repeated in all of Belarus's official documents and speeches, it is never footnoted or referenced in any way, and even Belarusian scientists confess that they have no idea what its source is. A Belarusian radioecologist told me that he even made a special effort to find out where the number came from but got nowhere.

Instead, one international study that also included Belarusian scientists concluded that 33 percent of Chernobyl's cesium fell on Belarus, which is probably a good measure of the total amount of radionuclides that descended on the country.

One-third is nevertheless a large amount, but the explanation that so much fell on Belarus because of the prevailing winds is as unsatisfying as efforts to find the source of the 70 percent claims.

For one thing, the dirtiest territories were in the *eastern* part of Belarus, around the towns of Gomel— Belarus's third-largest city—and Mogilev, 180 miles to the northeast. But at the time of the explosion on April 26, 1986, ground-level winds were blowing south towards Kiev, while atmospheric winds a thousand meters high— where the graphite fire's smokestack effect lifted a good part of the radioactivity—went through *western* Belarus and arrived in northeastern Poland on April 27. From there the radioactive wind went on to Finland and

Sweden, where it set off alarms at the Forsmark nuclear power plant north of Stockholm.

A light ground-level breeze shifted towards Gomel on the 27th, but the reactor's release of radionuclides had dropped significantly by then, as had the force of their expulsion from the core. So it seems unlikely that either was sufficient to blow the contamination to Gomel. Atmospheric winds shifted in the city's direction on the 28th, but by the time the release of radionuclides increased significantly on May 1, both ground-level and atmospheric winds were directed south. In short, wind direction does not explain the causes of the extent of Belarus's contamination.

Rain was a likelier culprit. Soviet newspapers traced Belarus's contamination to heavy rains on April 28, which would have brought the radionuclides down when atmospheric winds were directed towards Gomel. Others maintain that the Soviet government seeded clouds to prevent rain from falling over the Chernobyl area. Still others claim that the clouds were seeded to bring radioactivity down on Belarus instead of letting it get to Moscow. Whatever the reason, a huge amount of radioactive rain fell on the country.

> "Judging which of the three most affected countries suffered the most is not straightforward and the figures are often confusing."

Confusing and Contradictory Numbers

Judging which of the three most affected countries suffered the most is not straightforward and the figures are often confusing. For example, the disaster removed 1 million hectares of Ukrainian farmlands and forests from service compared to 464,000 hectares in Belarus. By that criterion, Ukraine's economic loss might seem greater. In fact, Belarus suffered the smallest total amount of contaminated land. Russia—which rarely rates as much attention as Belarus and Ukraine—suffered the most, largely in the Bryansk region neighboring Belarus and in

the Kaluga-Tula-Orel region 300 miles northeast of the reactor.

Consider that all three countries define land as "contaminated" if cesium-137 levels on a square kilometer of land exceed one curie. But one curie is a relatively low amount of radioactivity when it is spread over such a large area. Natural background radioactivity from radon gas is between one and five curies in many inhabited parts of the world. So some of the contaminated lands are, relatively speaking, not really very radioactive.

Disparate outcomes for nations hit by Chernobyl's radiation make difficult the determination of which one got the worst of it. (Viktor Drachev/AFP/ Getty Images.)

Nevertheless, this means that there are 43,500 contaminated square kilometers in Belarus, 59,300 in Russia, and 53,500 in Ukraine. Thus, using the one-curie criterion, Belarus suffered the least and Russia suffered the most. But what do such figures really mean given the vast differences in size and contamination levels between the three countries? Belarus's contaminated lands amount to 23 percent of its total territory; Ukraine's, 5 percent; and Russia's 1.5. Moreover, if 24 percent of all the cesium that Chernobyl released fell on Russia, 20 percent on Ukraine, and another 20 percent on Europe, then fully one-third—33 percent—blanketed Belarus. And because Belarus's contamination was concentrated in a smaller area, radiation levels and exposures were higher.

Yet a different picture emerges when looked at in terms of human suffering. Altogether over the years, Ukraine evacuated and resettled 163,000 people—more than Belarus's 135,000 and far more than Russia's 52,000. This occurred because the parts of Ukraine contaminated with the 15 to 40 or more curies that mandate evacuation were more densely populated than similar regions in Belarus and Russia.

Of course, the flip side of not evacuating people is that they continue to live on contaminated territories. Leading in this category are 1.8 million people in Russia, followed by 1.5 million in Belarus and 1.1 million in Ukraine. There are more Chernobyl[-related] thyroid cancer cases in Belarus than in Ukraine and fewest in Russia. But Ukraine contributed the vast majority of the cleanup workers known as liquidators.

So, there really is no correct answer to the question of which country suffered most from Chernobyl. It all depends on what criterion you are using, as shown below. By nearly every measure, though, Belarus surely suffered greatly.

- **Russia**   Greatest amount of contaminated land
- **Ukraine**   Greatest number of people exposed to radiation
    Highest levels of contamination
    Inheritance of the Sarcophagus [protective cover put on reactor] and radioactive waste dumps
- **Belarus**   Greatest percentage of affected land and people relative to total national territory and population
    Highest percentage of total radionuclides released
    Greatest number of thyroid cancer cases

Russian and Belarusian Officials Continue to Minimize the Impact of Chernobyl

Yelena Starovoitova

Yelena Starovoitova is a journalist living in the former Soviet Union. In the following viewpoint she documents how Russian and Belarusian news media and government officials continue to downplay the severity of the 1986 accident at Chernobyl, which a former Russian minister of atomic energy characterized as "a minor technical incident" in 2001. The author argues that this is a concerted campaign fueled by a strong nuclear lobby looking to retain their profitability and by governments determined to decrease their expenditures on ongoing cleanup efforts and compensation to those hurt by the radiation released during and following the explosion and fire. As a result of this campaign, many Russians and Belarusians now doubt that there are any real lingering effects from Chernobyl and believe that symptoms are either psychosomatic delusions or the invention of cleanup workers looking for easy money.

On the eve of the 15th anniversary of the biggest man-made disaster in history—the explosion of the No. 4 unit at the Chernobyl nuclear power plant—Aleksei Yablokov, president of the Russian Environmental Policy Center, held a press conference at which he talked about the effects and lessons of the accident, as well as the fact that most people living in contaminated areas have already forgotten Chernobyl.

The causes of the accident are still disputed, and it is unclear how much nuclear fuel the exploding reactor released, Yablokov said. Attempts to calculate the number of people affected by the accident are still being made, and estimates range from hundreds of thousands to tens of millions. . . . Russia's former minister of atomic energy, Yevgeny Adamov, has said in interviews with foreign newspapers that the accident claimed only 28 lives and adversely affected no more than 2,000 children and adults. "In terms of number of victims, this was a minor technical incident." he said.

Because of statements like this, people are starting to forget Chernobyl and discount its effects, but that is a big mistake, the press conference organizers feel. Many people have started believing that the illnesses caused by the accident were invented by cleanup participants and people in communities near the power plant as a way of getting more money out of the government. In fact, however, official medical statistics show that almost everyone living in Bryansk Province and almost all those who took part in cleaning up the biggest man-made disaster in his-

> "[Russia] has not learned anything from Chernobyl."

tory are chronically ill (their health is almost completely ruined). Their children get sick more often and have more health problems than average—as do the parents. Biologists have proven that radiation can affect the human genome and mutations can be passed on from generation to generation, so people in Russia, Ukraine and Belarus will be feeling the effects of this terrible disaster for decades to come. After the accident, a sharp rise in infant mortality, cancer and thyroid disease was reported. Another terrible effect of Chernobyl is that half the children born in the irradiated parts of Ukraine show delayed mental development. . . .

Growing Costs and Increasing Risks

By 2000, some $300 billion to $360 billion had been spent on efforts to minimize the effects of the accident, and by 2015 the cost will hit $560 billion, many times more than any possible financial return from the use of atomic energy.

Russia currently has three nuclear power plants with RBMK reactors [such as the one at Chernobyl]: Smolensk, Kursk and Leningrad. None of them meets present-day international atomic energy safety standards, according to Vladimir Kuznetsov, director of the Russian Green Cross's nuclear and radiation safety program. Our country has not learned anything from Chernobyl, he says. Over the past 10 years, there have been 1,188 problems reported at nuclear power plants. There have also been more than 40 major incidents that resulted in small amounts or radiation being released into the environment. . . .

Biggest Bluff of the Century

Fifteen years after the accident at the Chernobyl nuclear power plant, the number of questions has only increased. The main one—what should be done?—has many answers. Debates continue to rage. . . .

Chernobyl is an epic, a story that can hardly be told in full in a single article (or even a book). There are the evacuees returning to their native villages behind barbed wire. There are the wild animals that have moved into abandoned buildings. There are the adventure-seeking tourists who are willing to risk their health for the sake of thrills and excitement. . . . But most of all, there is death—death that is invisible and hence all the more horrible.

> The nuclear lobby claims that mass hysteria over what happened is being fanned by oil and gas companies in an effort to eliminate competition.

"Chernobyl is the biggest bluff of the 20th century." This viewpoint also exists and is being expressed publicly. The International Atomic Energy Agency, whose prestige was badly shaken after April 26, 1986, is especially interested in promoting this view. . . .

Illnesses Are Psychosomatic

The nuclear lobby claims that mass hysteria over what happened is being fanned by oil and gas companies in an effort to eliminate competition. . . . To all their opponents' arguments about increased mortality and morbidity as a result of the Chernobyl accident, they have a brief response: "It hasn't been proven!" This is how the most inveterate and cynical criminals usually deny their crimes. But facts are a stubborn thing, unfortunately. In the years that have passed since the accident, one-fifth of the 150,000 Belarusians who took part in the cleanup have died. They were mainly able-bodied people between the ages of 40 and 50.

Could it be, as some nuclear industry officials maintain, that this is all a result of self-induced hypnosis? But then how can one explain the catastrophic increase in morbidity among unknowing young children? According to UN statistics, mortality among new-borns in Belarus has risen by 250%. Nine out of 10 children living in the

Former Russian Atomic Energy Minister Yevgeny Adamov described the Chernobyl catastrophe as "a minor technical incident." (Atta Kenare/ AFP/Getty Images.)

"zone" have health problems. It is predicted that the incidence of thyroid cancer will peak in 2005–2010. . . .

Whereas in relatively lucky Vitebsk Province, statistics show about one cancer death per 10,000 people, in the "Chernobyl" provinces of Mogilev and Gomel, the figures for cancer deaths are 19.3 and 39, respectively. But there are unsafe places in other regions as well. Eighteen villages approximately 50 kilometers from Minsk are in the zone of radioactive contamination. Every year, the death rate there is three to four times higher than the birthrate. The deaths are mainly among men between the ages of 35 and 45. The health of the next generation is most aptly characterized by the fact that many children are unable to do quality work for the duration of a single class period.

Radiation not only causes various types of cancer, it also weakens a person's immune system. As a result, he loses his resistance to diabetes and to cardiovascular, gastrointestinal and other diseases, which develop and progress without encountering effective resistance from the body. . . .

> "A year after he came to power, [Belarusian president Aleksander] Lukashenko abolished almost all compensation payments for cleanup workers."

Downplaying Severity to Save Money

The Belarusian government is watching all these processes with indifference. As residents of contaminated areas say, "They remember us only on the anniversary of the accident." . . .

In 1991, the Supreme Soviet passed a law on social protection for citizens affected by the Chernobyl disaster. A year after he came to power, Belarus' [president Aleksander] Lukashenko abolished almost all compensation payments for cleanup workers. . . . Even though the Constitution Court ruled the decree illegal, the benefits have still not been reinstated. . . .

Speaking to deputies to the [Russian] State Duma, [Lukashenko] stated that 2.5% of Belarus's budget is spent on Chernobyl programs. This actually *was* the case, but only before Lukashenko won the presidential election. In 1995, the treasury allocated $182 million for dealing with the aftermath of the Chernobyl accident, but in 2001 it allocated only $48 million, which is less than 2% of all government spending. . . .

In 1999, the Belarusian leadership decided it would be a good idea to review the permissible levels of radioactive contamination in food products and set new ones. Now the level for milk is 2.2 times higher than in Russia and Ukraine. The levels for water and meat are 2.3 and 3.7 times higher respectively. . . .

So it turns out that, despite loud statements from government rostrums, Belarus's Chernobyl victims have been left to fend for themselves. Their plights has become small change that the powers that be use in their games. The residents of the contaminated areas have essentially been turned into guinea pigs on which a large-scale experiment in survival is being conducted.

The Chernobyl Disaster Was the Fatal Blow to the USSR

Stephen Weeks

Stephen Weeks is a British author, filmmaker, conservationist, and radio commentator. He often writes for the *Prague Post*, the Czech Republic's English-language newspaper. During the Cold War, the Czech Republic was part of Czechoslovakia, a satellite nation of the Soviet Union and, in practice, controlled by Moscow.

In the following viewpoint, Weeks contextualizes the Chernobyl accident as experienced by individuals in various parts of Europe. The severity of the accident and its botched recovery forced Soviet leaders to reach out to Western nations, such as the United States, for aid. Weeks argues that this vastly accelerated the opening of the Soviet Union to Western ideas and interests. Although the Chernobyl accident did not directly trigger the collapse of the Soviet Union, Weeks explains that it did contribute to a worldwide sense that the regime was

SOURCE. Stephen Weeks, "Chernobyl: The Day the Empire Cracked," *The Prague Post*, April 19, 2006. Copyright © Prague Post, spol. s.r.o. All rights reserved. Reproduced by permission.

insupportably corrupt, giving a boost to existing democratization movements throughout the Eastern bloc.

"I remember it very well . . . when it happened," said a friend who was in his teens when the Chernobyl nuclear reactor blew in 1986. "I was picking cherries that afternoon."

Cherries? In April? The disaster happened April 26, 1986, but the Czech government didn't officially announce it until several months later. A mother I spoke to remembers her daughter, then age 6, running in the rain outside their house, mouth upturned to the sky and then saying how she thought the raindrops were "sandy" and tasted salty.

The nuclear cloud passed over the country, but the authorities kept quiet. Only those who listened to Voice of America [an international broadcasting service funded by the U.S. government] or the BBC [British Broadcasting Corporation] or who worked in certain professions with access to environmental information had any idea. That summer was great for mushrooms. A neighbor of that mother had picked so many she had to wash them in the bath. Presumably they hardly needed cooking in the microwave.

I was in the United States when it happened and flew home to Wales wondering if there would be a Europe to fly back to. I do remember, about three years later, stumbling on a small graveyard in the mountains of North Wales, finding a row of babies' graves; they had all been born a few months after Chernobyl—and had all died at less than 18 months old.

In this country [the Czech Republic], in November 1986, the male birthrate plunged. Male embryos are more sensitive to chem-

> Chernobyl was more than a single disaster. . . . It was the first highly visible crack in the Soviet Union.

ical and environmental stress during the third month of development than females.

In North Wales, where the cloud had passed into the high hills, there are many farms where sheep pastures are still contaminated by Chernobyl fallout. In the United Kingdom as a whole, 20 years afterward, there are still nearly 400 farms with more than 200,000 contaminated sheep.

The hammer-and-sickle emblem of the fallen Soviet Union crowns a building in the abandoned city of Pripyat. (Daniel Berehulak/Getty Images.)

More than a Single Disaster

But Chernobyl was more than a single disaster, however large that one event was. It was the first highly visible crack in the Soviet Union. Things would never again be the same for the evil empire. The West had known the bitter truth of Soviet life for many years before: the 500,000 prisoners in the East, in Siberia, as an example, the repressive regimes in the satellite states—all that, but none of it actually affected us in the West personally. Indeed, there was even the feeling that the Russian people had always been victims, and that somehow that could never change. That was their destiny.

But suddenly in April 1986 the tragedy of life in the Soviet Union directly threatened us. Even after Swedish scientists had sounded the alarm, for 48 hours after the explosion the Soviet News Agency Tass was putting out, "Everything is absolutely safe and there is no need to worry; the accident is under control."

The staff of the power plant were at first too frightened to tell their superiors, hoping that somehow they could patch it up themselves. Only two months before the accident, Ukrainian Energy Minister Vitaly Sklyarov had stated that the odds of a meltdown were one in 10,000—and that the Chernobyl plant had strict, reliable controls and three safety systems to prevent an accident. There was a deadly delay in evacuating the area. When the decision was finally made, 50,000 people were moved out in a single afternoon.

> Chernobyl was the landmark event, the symbolic and de facto beginning of the end of Soviet communism.

I remember watching CNN's coverage of the event. The most extraordinary moment was when the Soviet Union realized it couldn't handle the disaster. Ukraine had been, centuries before, the heart of Russian culture. It was one of the founding republics of the Soviet Union, joining in 1921. For all intents and purposes, it was Russia. The year before, in 1985, Mikhail Gorbachev had become first secretary of the Communist Party. In the United States, President Ronald Reagan was pressing ahead with his "Strategic Defense Initiative," the SDI—popularly known as Star Wars—which had been announced in 1984.

Chernobyl was the climb-down: the first time the Soviet Union had to admit its bankrupt society to the world. Admission is hardly the word, as it was self-evident. The West was actually invited to assist—which it was anxious to do to save its own skin—and the dark secrecy of the Soviet era was exposed.

In November 1986, at the arms limitation summit, Reagan scored a considerable victory over Gorbachev when he made it clear that the United States was prepared to out-spend the USSR with Star Wars. Within two years of Chernobyl, Perestroyka [political reforms initiated by Gorbachev] was in full swing, and the first private/state real estate developments with U.S. partners were beginning in Moscow—something that would have seemed unthinkable prior to the accident.

The Beginning of the End

The exposure of the emptiness of the Soviet threat, as Chernobyl demonstrated, had ripple effects all over the satellite countries. In Prague, speculation was rife that the regime couldn't last, but no one would attempt to guess how long it could survive in its death throes.

Some said it might hang on for another 10 or 20 years. The police were still aggressive in pursuing dissidents, and yet there were signs that the writing on the wall was evident. . . .

An academic found, to his surprise, that he was allowed out of the country to attend a conference in the United States in 1987—something he had been denied before.

When he returned, the books he had acquired on his visit were, as he had expected, confiscated. However, three weeks later, a policeman delivered them to his home, saying they had been cleared. The officer was very particular to leave his name, as if trying to establish his good credentials for when the time came.

"But what made me convinced the end was near," my academic friend said, "was that the rabid communists began to privatize a lot of businesses throughout

Czechoslovakia. . . . They began to steal in earnest before the regime closed."

I contend that Chernobyl was the landmark event, the symbolic and de facto beginning of the end of Soviet communism.

The regimes would have ended anyhow, of course: Their lies could not have survived the Internet; the great Czechoslovak infrastructure that the communists had taken over in 1948 was simply worn-out by the 1980s; movements like Solidarity in Poland [the first non-Communist trade union in a Communist European nation] were well established. But Chernobyl was a worldwide event. It gave the focus for a swifter end.

Today [in 2006], the plant at Chernobyl is at the center of many thousands of acres that have remained depopulated and have become an unnatural nature reserve. Although the old communist statistics stated that only 49 people were killed in the accident, it is thought that up to 40,000 Ukrainians were exposed to and suffered from the residual affects of radiation.

The international spotlight that was suddenly put on Chernobyl turned into the torch of Central Europe's freedom.

Farming in the Contaminated Zones of Belarus

Steven Lee Myers

In 2004 Belarusian president Aleksandr Lukashenko declared that some of Belarus's contaminated regions could be opened to farming and other economic development. Although this announcement was in accordance with findings by the United Nations' World Health Organization and International Atomic Energy Agency, it was still highly controversial.

According to Steven Lee Myers—the author of the following viewpoint and the former Moscow news bureau chief for the *New York Times*—Lukashenko's government worked hand-in-hand with international agencies, such as the United Nations Development Programme, to improve farming techniques, limit contamination of foodstuffs, and cautiously move forward in returning Belarus's tainted territory to productive use. Nonetheless, Myers points out, although there are regulations and oversight for commercial operations, private gardens,

---

SOURCE. Steven Lee Myers, "Belarus Resumes Farming in Chernobyl Radiation Zone," *The New York Times*, October 22, 2005. Copyright © 2005 by The New York Times Company. Reproduced by permission. www.nytimes.com.

hunting, fishing, and wild foraging—significant food sources for much of this country's impoverished population—are generally unregulated and often toxic.

The winter rye is already sprouting green in the undulating fields of the state cooperative farm here. The summer's crop—rye, barley and rapeseed—amounted to 1,400 tons. Best of all, the farm's director, Vladimir I. Pryzhenkov, said, none of it tested radioactive.

That is progress. The farm's 4,000 acres are nestled among some of the most contaminated spots on earth, the poisoned legacy of the worst nuclear accident in history: the explosion at Chernobyl Reactor No. 4 on April 26, 1986.

Nearly a quarter of Belarus, including some of its prime farmland, remains radioactive to some degree. Mr. Pryzhenkov's farm represents part of the government's efforts to put the contaminated lands back to good use.

The farm, no longer known as the Karl Marx collective but still state-owned, reopened [in 2003] with the millions of dollars' worth of harvesters, tractors and other equipment provided by President Aleksandr G. Lukashenko's government.

A year before that the checkpoints that once restricted access to this region, 150 miles from Chernobyl, disappeared. Families began returning. Some had never left; all needed jobs.

Mr. Pryzhenkov, assigned here from another co-op in what he called "a promotion," has also begun breeding horses and cattle for beef, though not for milk. Milk produced here would be far too dangerous for human consumption.

"This was all falling apart," he said as he drove a battered UAZ jeep over the farm's muddy, rutted roads. "There was nothing for the people to do here."

Time to Revive the Region

Mr. Lukashenko, a former collective farm boss himself, declared [in 2004] that it was time to revive the contaminated regions, outlining a vision of new homes and villages, of new industry, of rejuvenated farms. "Land should work for the country," he said.

> Lands where agriculture was banned or severely restricted can be safe for growing crops again . . . using techniques to minimize the absorption of radioactive particles into produce.

His authoritarian decrees, on this and other topics, have prompted shock, fear and even ridicule, but a scientific study released in September [2005] by seven United Nations agencies and the World Bank more or less agreed with him.

It concluded that Chernobyl's lasting effects on health and the environment had not proved as dire as first predicted. It recommended that the authorities in Russia, Ukraine and Belarus take steps to reverse psychological trauma caused by Chernobyl, encouraging investment and redevelopment.

Lands where agriculture was banned or severely restricted can be safe for growing crops again, the report said, using techniques to minimize the absorption of radioactive particles into produce.

"It is desirable to identify sustainable ways to make use of the most affected areas that reflect the radiation hazard but also revive the economic potential for the benefit of the community," the report said.

Its conclusions have stirred controversy. Greenpeace denounced it as a whitewash. Even a member of Mr. Lukashenko's government, Valery L. Gurachevsky, the scientific director of Belarus's committee on Chernobyl, called parts of the report "too optimistic."

But here in the countryside, where entire villages were left to rot in an invisible scourge, the report's underlying principle is a welcome one. Gennadi V. Kruzhayev, now 38, had just begun working on the Karl Marx col-

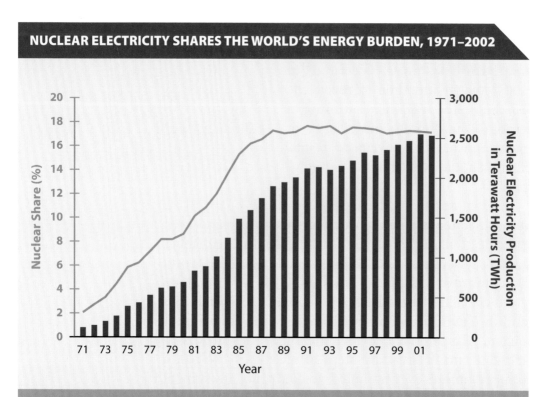

NUCLEAR ELECTRICITY SHARES THE WORLD'S ENERGY BURDEN, 1971–2002

Taken from: "Nuclear Power in the World Today," World-Nuclear.org, March 2009.

lective when the accident occurred. He has since drifted from job to job. He drove a taxi. He pumped gas. One day recently he was atop a tractor, plowing the black earth for next spring's sowing.

"The main thing," he said, "is to have jobs."

"Off-Limits" Areas Routinely Ignored

The Chernobyl disaster spewed radioactive material over all of Europe, but naturally the closest areas—Russia, Ukraine and Belarus, then Soviet republics—suffered the worst.

The Soviet authorities declared an emergency exclusion zone within 19 miles of the reactor, a circle straddling the border between Ukraine and Belarus. The zone remains closed, except to the workers overseeing the reactor's decontamination, a few hard-luck pensioners who have drifted back and, increasingly, curious tourists on macabre day trips.

The contamination—particularly from cesium-137 as well as the more deadly strontium-90 and plutonium—was hardly confined to that circle, though. Areas as radioactive as parts of the exclusion zone still appear on maps of Belarus as irregular splashes across the eastern part of the country.

Those areas remain off limits, at least in theory. Around them are areas with lower levels, creating a patchwork of go and no-go zones that by all appearances are routinely ignored.

More than 130,000 Belarussians were relocated in the years after Chernobyl, but mostly to areas with lower levels of contamination, often only a few miles away. About 1.3 million people, or 14 percent of the population, live in contaminated areas, though officials say that with certain precautions, they face little health risk.

In those areas farming never stopped entirely, though the economy collapsed. Instead, the state's farms adopted measures to minimize contamination of crops, including the use of certain fertilizers. Some crops absorb less radiation anyway; those that absorb more are grown only for fodder.

> Mr. Lukashenko's government . . . has worked with international agencies . . . to improve crop yields and limit contamination of food products.

Reclamation Proceeds Slowly

Since Mr. Lukashenko came to power in 1994, the government has tried to expand agriculture in the region, removing restrictions on less contaminated areas. Gennadi V. Antsipov, who oversees reclamation for the country's Chernobyl committee, said the process was complicated and, despite Mr. Lukashenko's urgings, deliberate.

With the decree "Land should work for the country," Belarus President Alexander Lukashenko ordered farming's resumption in contaminated areas of his nation. (Viktor Drachev/AFP/Getty Images.)

Of 1,000 square miles of contaminated land, only 54 square miles has so far been returned to active agricultural use, including Viduitsy. A periodic survey completed [in 2004] found that still more land could be reclaimed.

"Why should we rush this issue?" Mr. Antsipov said in the capital, Minsk. "It is like sending someone to the moon just to prove we can colonize it."

Mr. Lukashenko's government, despite its diplomatic isolation, has worked with international agencies, including the United Nations Development [Programme], to improve crop yields and limit contamination of food products. "We are trying to provide people a fishing rod, not a fish as we did before," Valery Y. Shevchuk, the Chernobyl committee's deputy chairman, said.

Many Foods Still Radioactive

Radioactive materials, especially cesium-137, with a half-life of 30 years, will decay over time, but life in the contaminated parts of Belarus will not soon be normal.

In Viduitsy, Mr. Pryzhenkov pointed out the fields that remained too hot to grow even animal fodder. They are fairly obvious because they are overgrown, though he sometimes consults a map. With precautions, he and others say, the food grown here is safe. The government claims to strictly check all produce; without a certificate, farmers cannot sell what they grow.

Other risks lurk in the forests and fields. Small kitchen gardens, used as in Soviet times for subsistence, are mostly unregulated.

Mushrooms and berries, as well as wild game, absorb high levels of radiation. Fish from local lakes and rivers are toxic. Keeping bees for honey is not considered a good idea. Government advisories warn people not to eat those delicacies.

Vera A. Brausova, 73, who lives in a village called Krasny Kurgan, does anyway. Asked about health concerns, she explained that she had lived through World War II, the Chernobyl accident and a fire that burned down the first house she was evacuated to.

"What health are you talking about?" she said.

Children Harmed by the Chernobyl Accident Should Be Helped at Home

Sarah Carey

Sarah Carey is an Irish columnist for the *Sunday Times* (of London, England). In the following viewpoint, Carey takes issue with the Chernobyl Children's Project International (CCPI), a United Nations–accredited international developmental organization founded by the Irish peace and humanitarian worker Adi Roche. Although CCPI funds many programs, their most prominent effort pays for sick Belarusian children to take recuperative vacations, often to Ireland.

Although Carey does not question Roche's good intentions, she nonetheless expresses serious concerns about the efficacy of Roche's methods. According to Carey, not only do these vacations (and the fundraising that supports them) perpetuate the psychologically crippling myth that most illness in Belarus is a

SOURCE. Sarah Carey, "Chernobyl Children Should be Offered Help at Home," *Sunday Times*, September 7, 2008, p. 14. Copyright © 2008 Sunday Times. Reproduced by permission.

direct result of the Chernobyl disaster, but also divert funds that could be spent improving conditions in Belarus year-round, as opposed to giving some children a brief respite from Belarusian poverty.

How can you criticise Adi Roche? . . . Her Chernobyl Children's Project has harnessed the goodwill, money and energy of hundreds of equally well-meaning, generous families who host [Belarusian] children's holidays here [in Ireland].

So how do you tell Roche and those families that their project is capable of harm, and that there are better ways to help those needy children? Gently, but firmly. It is time to state bluntly that the story of the Chernobyl Children's Project is not a simple one of a fairy godmother saving the lives of sick children. The story of Chernobyl is considerably more complex than the one we perceive every time a plane full of pale, cancer-stricken children lands in Ireland.

Roche has described as shocking the decision by the Belarusian government to prevent children travelling to Ireland, or other host countries, for an annual holiday. The ban is an overreaction, and international pressure may have it overturned. But the Belarusians have a point.

Their ban was provoked by the failure of Tanya Kazyra, 16, who was on her ninth and last visit to a family in California, to board a return flight from San Francisco on August 5. She told the Associated Press: "I love my motherland and my grandmother. However, my life there is hard. And I have a family here." Who could blame her? Belarus is a poor country, still devastated by the aftermath of the fire at the Chernobyl nuclear power station in 1986. When children from there are brought to a rich western environment for a few weeks, and showered with the best of everything we have to offer—

Photo on previous page: Some people question how helpful the philanthropic endeavors of Adi Roche may be for the creation of the Chernobyl Children's Project International (CCPI) organization. (Tom Stoddart/ Getty Images) medical treatment, sympathy, nice food, new clothes and toys—is it any wonder they do not want to go back? How can they face returning to their old lives once they have seen that the faraway hills are very green indeed?

> The legacy of Chernobyl is not one of congenital deformities and childhood leukaemias, but of a nation cursed by the label of victimhood.

Few Orphans Victims of Chernobyl

The Irish government would be rightly annoyed if a well-intentioned American philanthropist took children out of Temple Street hospital to Florida or California, showed them Disneyland and showered them with treats, and then the kids refused to come home. Giving them a holiday seems like a charitable act, but Adi Roche has to face a number of realities. The first is that, contrary to popular belief, the World Health Organisation (WHO) has conclusively proven that cancer rates and congenital abnormalities in Belarus are no higher than in other former Soviet Union states.

Whenever I share this information, people react with disbelief. The only story they know is that radiation poisoning has resulted in high rates of terrible cancers among Belarusians. But that myth was categorically debunked by the Chernobyl Forum report issued by the WHO in 2005. The report was compiled by a team of more than 100 scientists who attempted to quantify how many people died or became ill as a result of the Chernobyl fire.

They concluded that three groups of people were affected. There were the heroic emergency workers who fought the blaze, 56 of whom died from acute radiation sickness. There were thousands of children who, due to the complete mismanagement of the crisis by the Belarusian government, were allowed to continue drinking contaminated milk from the region. Some 4,000 children contracted thyroid cancer as a result. Most of those were treated successfully, but eight did not survive. The third group affected is the general population, which has suffered devastating long-term damage to their mental but not physical health. The legacy of Chernobyl is not one of congenital deformities and childhood leukaemias, but of a nation cursed by the label of victimhood. Belarusians suffer acute anxiety, and any illness, miscarriage or medical setback is attributed to radiation instead of the general misery of life. They have been struck by what the WHO forum report called "paralysing fatalism". What they need is help to get on with their lives, not encouragement to believe that which is simply not true—that radiation continues to result in excessive cancers and illness.

Improve Everyday Lives Instead

That said, Belarus is a poor country and many of its children are in need. But I believe Roche's efforts are misguided. If [the humanitarian group] Concern started flying plane loads of African children here for a month every summer, people would quite rightly question the wisdom of such a strategy. Yes, those children would get a boost from good food and medical treatment. But then what? It is illogical, unsustainable and a poor use of resources to bring a child on holiday for a few weeks. It is clearly much more sensible and in the long-term interests of the child to improve their quality of life at home for every week of the year.

> Belarusian childcare workers . . . do their best with poor resources. . . . They need washing machines and cookers, proper showers and playgrounds.

There are other charities in Ireland who are quietly and effectively doing that. But you may not know about them because they don't pose with deformed children in front of television cameras—a practice that most leading international charities abhor.

Tom McEnaney, the former Irish business editor of [the *Sunday Times* of London], has been visiting Belarus for over 10 years with the International Orphanage Development Programme (IODP), which has worked with all 60 orphanages in Belarus. The only reason I know about the project is because he's a friend of mine. Publicity is not high on his agenda.

McEnaney observes that every time a new member of the group comes to Belarus, they are shocked to discover that the children are quite healthy. That's because Irish people have been conditioned to expect missing limbs and terrible deformities. They are surprised to find that Belarusian children look very like ours.

McEnaney praises Belarusian childcare workers who do their best with poor resources. He believes the children's needs are, simply, "capital". They need washing machines and cookers, proper showers and playgrounds. The IODP buys farm machinery and improves storage houses so that orphanages can grow their own food. They buy new beds and blankets locally, in order to give the economy a boost. It's not emotive, but it's effective and sustainable. Roche could perhaps learn something from this practice. I believe she has good intentions but a bad policy. She should consider helping Belarusian children in their own country, and she should tell them the full truth about Chernobyl.

A Comparison of the Chernobyl and Three Mile Island Incidents

Richard D. Fitzgerald

In this viewpoint, Richard D. Fitzgerald compares the two major social philosophies of the twentieth century—free-market capitalism and scientific socialism—and contrasts two major twentieth-century atomic energy disasters: the 1979 partial core meltdown at the Three Mile Island nuclear facility near Harrisburg, Pennsylvania, and the 1986 explosion and meltdown at Chernobyl's reactor 4 in Ukraine.

The author argues that each accident was the result of the prominent social philosophy of the nation where it occurred. Ever-increasing demand for material gains in the United States drove reckless development of ever more productive power plants (although the damage caused by the Three Mile Island accident was mitigated by another aspect of capitalist society:

SOURCE. Richard D. Fitzgerald, *Science and Its Times: Understanding the Social Significance of Scientific Discovery, vol. 7.* Belmont, CA: Gale, 2001. Copyright © 2001 Gale Group. Copyright © 2005, Thomson Gale, a part of The Thomson Corporation. Reproduced by permission of Gale, a part of Cengage Learning.

a free and open press), while the rigidity of autocratic Soviet culture both masked the dangers of the Chernobyl plant and made it impossible for Soviets to properly inform their population or request international aid once the terrible scope of the accident became apparent.

The success of industrialization was the result of the energy revolution. Energy is the force or power that is needed to accomplish a particular task. Over time, energy sources have evolved significantly. The earliest form of energy used by humans was muscle power from themselves or animals. This situation progressed with successful attempts at harnessing the power of water and the wind, which increased the amount of energy humans could utilize but were very unreliable. The first major breakthrough came with the invention of the steam engine.

Steam power drove the pursuit of materialistic utility until World War I, when petroleum replaced it as the energy of choice. Oil was used to drive the combustion engine. This device was small, powerful, and had both peacetime and military applications. Petroleum, a fossil fuel, has a finite supply and is unequally distributed around the world. Petroleum has thus changed the global geopolitical situation; areas such as the Middle East have become important because of their oil reserves.

> Two economic, political, and social philosophies dominated the world during most of the century—free market capitalism and scientific socialism.

In 1939 the first atomic chain reaction took place, and the world entered the nuclear age. This energy was not just viewed as a new weapon; many people believed that it could become an infinite source of power for domestic consumption.

This march toward utility, based upon a belief in humankind's ability to solve problems through the

> "A series of major technological disasters set in motion a process that would eventually begin not only a debate over the perceived infallibility of science and technology but also the ethical foundation of Enlightenment utility."

proper application of scientific and technological principles, did not operate in a vacuum. In the twentieth century, ideology began to dominate the quest for utility. Two economic, political, and social philosophies dominated the world during most of the century—free market capitalism and scientific socialism.

Capitalism vs. Socialism

During the Enlightenment [the eighteenth-century intellectual movement emphasizing rationality and individualism over tradition], free market capitalism was the economic system created in the quest for happiness. [British philosopher] Adam Smith, its founder, stated that in a free market people determine the goods and services to be produced. He believed that people would never act against their own best self-interest; thus, their economic energy would always be used in a positive way. The success of this philosophy, in turn, was to be measured in material prosperity.

The other economic model was constructed by [German philosopher] Karl Marx as an attack against the volatile and sometimes destructive forces of the free market. Originally known as scientific socialism, it stated that the true natural law of economics was one that promoted economic equality. This equality, in turn, would be established and guided by a strong revolutionary elite.

Both economic philosophies were grounded in the production and distribution of goods. As industrialization evolved in both systems, energy became an increasingly important factor. By the last half of the twentieth century, the pursuit of material utility began to strain the financial and energy resources of the world. By the early 1960s, many technologists believed that nuclear power

was the "wave of the future," while others argued that, at least initially, there would have to be a combination of nuclear and fossil fuel.

Disasters Under Each Philosophy

Beginning in 1979, however, a series of major technological disasters set in motion a process that would eventually begin not only a debate over the perceived infallibility of science and technology but also the ethical foundation of Enlightenment utility. March 28, 1979, was the first day in this new process. On that day, in a nuclear power plant called Three Mile Island, located in Pennsylvania, a series of errors—both mechanical and human—allowed water used to cool the plant's reactor to drain. This event caused the plant's radioactive core to overheat and begin to melt down, eventually consum-

Governmental attempts to control the flow of information followed both the Three Mile Island (above) and Chernobyl accidents. (**Bill Pierce/Time Life Pictures/Getty Images.**)

The Manhattan Project

The Manhattan Engineer District, a secret U.S. government project begun in 1942 to develop an atomic bomb, was managed by Brigadier General Leslie Groves and undertaken by the U.S. Army Corps of Engineers. Undertaken at the urging of physicists Leo Szilard, Eugene Wigner, Edward Teller, Enrico Fermi, and Albert Einstein, the project responded to the threat of atomic weapon development by Nazi Germany. Ultimately, the U.S. effort brought together intelligence operatives, leading physicists, chemists, and engineers, as well as thousands of managers and workers at four major sites.

The best known of these sites, Los Alamos, in New Mexico, was the scientific and design headquarters of the project. Directed by the physicist J. Robert Oppenheimer, the Los Alamos site developed the theoretical knowledge behind the bomb and pieced together the designs for the two types of devices used on the Japanese cities of Hiroshima—a uranium bomb (code-named Little Boy)—and Nagasaki—a plutonium device (code-named Fat Man)—in August 1945. . . .

Secrecy was the watchword of the project, both among workers and scientists. General Groves' system of compartmentalization meant that almost all project employees, military or civilian, had knowledge of only their small piece of the atomic puzzle, with no

ing a third of the core element. While proper steps were taken to avoid a major disaster, serious questions about the ultimate safety of nuclear energy took hold of the American consciousness.

Several years later, a nightmare scenario began halfway around the world from the United States in the territory of its major rival, the Soviet Union. On April 26, 1986, a major explosion occurred at the nuclear power plant at Chernobyl, which is in the Ukraine. The largest radiation disaster in history, the explosion created a cloud of cesium 137 and iodine 131 three miles high and ten times more radioactive than the one from the Hiroshima bomb. A total of 9,500 kilometers of land were contaminated in Byelorussia, Ukraine, and the Russian overview of how the entire project fit together. . . .

[On August 6, 1945 the U.S. dropped the first atomic bomb on Hiroshima, and dropped a second two days later on Nagasaki.] After the bombs' detonations, the wartime Japanese government, at the command of Emperor Hirohito, abandoned its plan for massive resistance to U.S. invasion and surrendered on August 14, 1945. The devastation of the bombing, which killed more than 60,000 in Hiroshima and more than 30,000 in Nagasaki, would become known only in the weeks to come. More than 100,000 people injured by the atomic bombs' blasts and radiation were forced to cope with its impact for the rest of their lives. . . .

The Project forever changed warfare, international relations, and America's sense of security. Atomic weapons in the hands of governments or terrorists created the possibility of a nuclear holocaust. That specter of mass destruction would not only affect America's defense policy but also help to shape the nation's postwar society and culture.

SOURCE. *Russell Olwell, "Manhattan Project," in* Americans at War, *edited by John Resch, vol. 3: 1901–1945. Detroit: Macmillan Reference USA, 2005.*

Federation. Twenty-eight people were killed outright, but eventually 650,000 would be affected by the radiation. This disaster was of apocalyptic proportions, and . . . its specter still haunts that area of [Eastern] Europe. Since the disaster, there has been a dramatic increase in thyroid cancer, along with a significant increase in illness and birth defects among newborns.

These two disasters refocused much of the energy community back to the use of fossil fuels. Once again the belief that technology could create cleaner, more productive engines helped breathe new life into the use of petroleum. On March 24, 1989, however, the super-tanker *Exxon Valdez* ran aground on Bligh Reef and spilled 11 million gallons of crude oil into Alaska's

> There is a tension between the absolute right of the individual to pursue happiness . . . and the rights of society to have a safe, clean environment.

Prince William Sound. This tragedy not only killed about 250,000 sea birds but also devastated the fishing industry in the entire area. . . .

The Impact of Ideology on Policy

In reaction to these disasters, people initially focused on the ideologies of the two participants. The rigid, oppressive, controlling nature of Marxist Leninism [communism developed by Vladimir Lenin in the USSR] was blamed for the Chernobyl disaster. The Soviet system proved incapable of containing the nuclear emergency. Once the accident occurred, moreover, the initial reaction of the totalitarian government was to control everything, including the flow of information. This decision allowed radiation to pollute most of the Soviet Union's neighbors.

In the United States, there was also an initial attempt to control information on the part of the government in both the Three Mile Island and Exxon disasters. A more open society with a free press eventually resulted in a release of information, but the capitalist system of the United States had also created the gluttonous appetite for material goods that had contributed to these disasters. The energy needs connected to satisfying the production levels required by this appetite have created one of the most important problems facing the American community today. Questions about how long the natural environment can withstand these types of violations are beginning to find an important place in U.S. civil debate.

The major philosophical problem in this situation revolves around the question of choice. There is a tension between the absolute right of the individual to pursue happiness (based upon the materialistic orientation of the Enlightenment's concept of utility) and the rights of society to have a safe, clean environment. The free market economy, which has over time raised a lifestyle based upon material acquisition to the level of a human right, is now being questioned. Many scientists believe that this model of mass consumption is not an environmentally sustainable one.

The Chernobyl Disaster Shows That Nuclear Energy Is Inherently Unsafe

Harvey Wasserman

Harvey Wasserman is a history professor, journalist, environmentalist, and author of a dozen books, including *Solartopia! Our Green-Powered Earth, A.D. 2030*. In the 1970s, Wasserman helped found the U.S. grassroots antinuclear movement, coining the phrase "No Nukes." He continues to serve as an advisor to Greenpeace USA and the Nuclear Information and Resource Service. In the following viewpoint, Wasserman takes Chernobyl as a primary example in arguing that nuclear energy is, fundamentally, a public safety, economic, and environmental nightmare. He rails against recent attempts to portray traditional and developing atomic energy technologies as "green," and insists that nuclear energy is a failed concept that must be entirely

SOURCE. Harvey Wasserman, "Chernobyl Reminds Us That Nukes Are NOT Green," *The Huffington Post*, April 28, 2007. Copyright © 2007 HuffingtonPost.com. Reproduced by permission of the author.

abandoned so that our resources can be sharply focused on a sustainable, efficient power-base of renewable energy.

Twenty-one years ago [on April 26, 1986], lethal radiation poured into the breezes over Europe and into the jet stream above, carrying death and disease around the planet.

It could be happening again as you read this: either by error, as at Chernobyl and Three Mile Island, or by terror, as could have happened on September 11, 2001.

Those who now advocate a "rebirth" of this failed technology forget what happened during these "impossible" catastrophes, or refuse to face their apocalyptic reality, both ecological and financial.

Radiation monitors in Sweden, hundreds of miles away, first detected the fallout from the blast at Chernobyl Unit 4. The reactor complex had just been extolled in the Soviet press as the ultimate triumph of a "new generation" in atomic technology.

The [Mikhail] Gorbachev government hushed up the accident, then reaped a whirlwind of public fury that helped bring down the Soviet Union. The initial silence in fact killed people who might otherwise have taken protective measures. In downtown Kiev, just 80 kilometers away, a parade of uninformed citizens—many of them very young—celebrated May Day amidst a hard rain of lethal fallout. It should never have happened.

Ten days after the explosion, radiation monitors at Point Reyes Station, on the California coast, detected that fallout. A sixty percent drop in bird births soon followed. (The researcher who made that public was fired).

Before they happened, reactor pushers said accidents like those at Three Mile Island [TMI] and Chernobyl were "impossible." But. . . .

To this day, no one knows how much radiation escaped from TMI, where it went or who it harmed.

A Near-Repeat of Chernobyl

A power failure [in] September [2000] disabled the cooling system at the Beloyarsk, Russia nuclear power plant, causing the radioactive core to overheat. Alexei Yablokov of the Center for Ecological Problems of Russia reports that "we were just half-an-hour from another Chernobyl." When plant operators went to turn on the emergency back-up diesel generators, they failed to start. It took 36 minutes to get the poorly maintained generators working. The problems at Beloyarsk triggered the shutdown of two reactors at a nearby high-security nuclear reprocessing facility. The Mayak facility was without power for 45 minutes. Plant official Vitaly Sadovnikov told the *Manchester Guardian* that only his staff's "near military discipline" avoided a more serious accident.

SOURCE. *"30 Minutes to Chernobyl,"* Earth Island Journal, Summer 2001.

But 2400 central Pennsylvanians who have sued to find out have been denied their day in court for nearly thirty years. The epithet "no one died at Three Mile Island" is baseless wishful thinking.

To this day also, no one knows how much radiation escaped from Chernobyl, where it went and who was harmed. Dr. Alexey Yablokov, former environmental advisor to the late [Russian] President Boris Yeltsin, and president of the Center for Russian Environmental Policy, estimates the death toll at 300,000. The infant death and childhood cancer rates in the downwind areas have been horrific. Visual images of the innumerable deformed offspring make the most ghastly science fiction movies seem tame.

Contemptible Claims of Safety

Industry apologists have stretched the limits of common decency to explain away these disasters. Patrick Moore, who falsely claims to be a founder of Greenpeace, has called TMI a "success story." An industry doctor long ago argued that Chernobyl would somehow "lower the cancer rate."

In human terms, such claims are beneath contempt. As one of the few reporters to venture into central Pennsylvania to study the health impacts of TMI, I can recall no worse experience in my lifetime than interviewing the scores of casualties.

The farmers made clear, with appalling documentation, that the animal death toll alone was horrendous. But the common human symptoms, ranging from a metallic taste the day of the accident to immediate hair loss, bleeding sores, asthma and so much more, came straight out of easily available literature from Hiroshima and Nagasaki.

There is no mystery about what happened downwind from TMI, only a conscious, well-funded corporate, media and judicial blackout.

At Chernobyl, the experience was repeated a thousand-fold. More than 800,000 (that's NOT a typo) Soviet draftees were run through the radioactive ruins as "jumpers," being exposed for 90 seconds or so to do menial clean-up work before hustling out. The ensuing cancer rate has been catastrophic (this huge cohort of very angry young men subsequently played a key role in bringing down the Soviet Union).

In both cases, "official" literature negating (at TMI) or minimizing (at Chernobyl) the death toll are utter nonsense. The multiple killing powers of radiation remain as much a

> "Those advocating more nukes ignore the myriad good reasons why no private insurance company has stepped forward to insure them against catastrophe."

medical mystery as how much fallout escaped in each case and where it went.

An Economic Nightmare

The economic impacts are not so murky. Moore's assertion that TMI was a success story is literally insane. A $900 million asset became a $2 billion clean-up job in a matter of minutes. At Chernobyl, the cost of the accident in lost power, damaged earth, abandoned communities and medical nightmares has been conservatively estimated at a half-trillion dollars, and still climbing.

The price of a melt-down or terror attack at an American nuke is beyond calculation. In most cases, reactors built in areas once far from population centers

A mourner leans against a monument dedicated to those who lost their lives from the Chernobyl blast on April 26, 1986. (Sergei Supinsky/ AFP/Getty Images.)

have now been surrounded by development, some of it bumping right up to the plant perimeters. Had the jets that hit the World Trade Center on 9/11/2001 instead hit Indian Point Units Two and Three, 45 miles north, the human and financial costs would have been unimaginable. Imagine the entire metropolitan New York area being made permanently uninhabitable, and then calculate out what happens to the US economy.

There remains no way to protect any of the roughly 450 commercial reactors on this planet from either terror attack or an error on the part of plant operators.

Those advocating more nukes ignore the myriad good reasons why no private insurance company has stepped forward to insure them against catastrophe. Those who say future accidents are impossible forget that exactly the same was said of TMI and Chernobyl.

The commercial fuel cycle *does* emit global warming in the uranium enrichment process. Uranium mining kills miners. [Uranium] milling leaves billions of tons of tailings [sandy waste material] that emit immeasurable quantities of radioactive radon. Regular reactor operations spew direct heat into the air and water. They also pump fallout into the increasingly populated surroundings, with impacts on the infant death rate that have already been measured and proven. And, of course, there is no solution for the management of high-level waste, a problem the industry promised would be solved a half-century ago.

A Failed Technology

Economically, early forays into a "new generation" of reactors have already been plagued by huge cost overruns and construction delays. At best they would take ten to fifteen years to build, by which time renewable sources and efficiency—which are already cheaper than new nukes—will have totally outstripped this failed technology. Small wonder Wall Street wants no part of this radioactive hype, which is essentially just another corporate campaign for taxpayer handouts.

This past Earth Day was an orgy of corporate green-washing, aided by the always-compliant major media, [that] tried to portray nukes as "green" energy. Nothing could be further from the truth.

We will never get to Solartopia, a sustainable economy based on renewables and efficiency, as long as atomic power sucks up our resources and threatens us with extinction.

Chernobyl Tourism

Tom Parfitt

Journalist Tom Parfitt has worked in Moscow since 2002 as a correspondent for several British newspapers. In the following viewpoint, he gives an overview of the evolving tourism industry centered on the Chernobyl reactor and the abandoned city of Pripyat.

In 2002, the radioactive Exclusion Zone surrounding the Chernobyl power plant was deemed safe enough to permit guided tours of the area. Since then, the popularity of such sightseeing trips has steadily grown, with thousands coming to view the remains of the reactor every year, and hundreds more to visit abandoned villages and Pripyat. Although Ukrainian officials and tour guides insist that radiation levels within the Exclusion Zone are generally "tolerable," the continued decay of the sarcophagus containing the remainder of reactor 4 and its nuclear fuel poses a constant risk of collapse.

SOURCE. Tom Parfitt, "Tourists Flock to the Dead Zone of Chernobyl," www.telegraph.co.uk, April 25, 2004. Copyright © Telegraph Media Group Limited 2004. Reproduced by permission.

Elk are among the wildlife that has reclaimed the area—known as the Exclusion Zone—evacuated after Chernobyl. (Patrick Landmann/Getty Images.)

Nearly 20 years after the world's worst nuclear disaster, the Chernobyl power plant and the poisonous wasteland that surrounds it has become an unlikely tourist destination.

Day-trippers armed with Geiger counters [used to detect radiation] take guided tours from Kiev through military checkpoints to the doorstep of the reactor. Increasing numbers of adventurers are finding their way into the irradiated zone, seeking the eerie thrill of entering family homes unchanged since they were evacuated at a few minutes' notice, two decades ago.

They sift through the abandoned homes of 48,000 workers and their families, whisked away as a veil of plutonium settled over the city. Family photographs, telephones, furniture upturned in the hasty departure, shoes, clothes and other belongings lie scattered through apartments.

Naturalists come to explore Chernobyl's "Garden of Eden"—the proliferation of greenery and wildlife that has sprung up in the exclusion zone around the ruined power station since the local population fled. More than 3,000 visitors go to the site every year, and hundreds more explore the abandoned villages in the 20-mile evacuated "dead zone".

> Tour agents say that there is no health risk from taking the trips.

"Strange as it may sound, people visit here from all over the world—the United States, Australia, Japan, the UK," said Yulia Marusich, an official guide who leads visitors to a viewing platform overlooking the concrete sarcophagus that encloses the remains of Reactor Four.

As she spoke, standing beside the sarcophagus, a Geiger counter began to tick frantically. It registered 50 times the natural background level of radiation—apparently a "tolerable" level of exposure for a short visit, officials say.

Engineers say that there is a serious risk that the sarcophagus could collapse, exposing hundreds of tons of unstable nuclear debris.

The Chernobyl catastrophe took place 18 years ago tomorrow, on April 26, 1986, when a powerful explosion destroyed the reactor, expelling a huge plume of radioactive dust that drifted across Europe.

Some 31 firefighters who fought the blaze were killed by massive doses of radiation, and thousands of civilians are thought to have died since from radiation-induced cancers. About 200 tons of concrete and other debris mixed with nuclear fuel are still trapped under the hastily-constructed concrete shell. Now, travel companies in Kiev are cashing in by charging day-trippers $190 for a tour of the disaster area in northern Ukraine.

Tourists can enter the dead zone, visit the ruined fourth unit, talk to villagers who returned to live in the area and see a graveyard of hundreds of trucks, helicop-

Nuclear Energy and the Environment

Nuclear energy has long been viewed as an alternative energy source to coal and petroleum, which are currently the principal sources of energy. Coal and petroleum provide efficient sources of energy, but their combustion also generates considerable carbon dioxide that escapes into the atmosphere. Although a few dissenters remain, the vast majority of climatologists hold that the build up of carbon dioxide in the atmosphere creates a greenhouse effect. This greenhouse effect dramatically warms the planet, which leads, in turn, to global climate change, resulting in different impacts on different regions of the planet.

Nuclear energy provides an especially attractive alternative to coal and petroleum because it does not contribute to the concentration of carbon dioxide in the atmosphere. Shifting to nuclear energy could potentially lead to a cleaner, healthier environment without a reduction in the human consumption of energy. However, the benefits of nuclear energy must be weighed against its substantial costs and risks. The principal cost of nuclear energy occurs with the safe disposal of radioactive wastes. In addition to the costs of disposal, there is the risk that nuclear radiation could be released into the environment, either at the

ters and armoured personnel vehicles which, according to brochures, are "so soaked with radiation that it is dangerous to approach".

Towns and villages that were evacuated in the days following the disaster are the biggest attraction—a time capsule from the late Soviet era. At Pripyat, two miles from the nuclear plant, communist banners painted for May 1—a date the city never greeted—are stacked in the back of a ruined theatre.

Tour agents say that there is no health risk from taking the trips. Areas of high radioactivity are marked off with triangular yellow signs. The journey involves passing through a series of military roadblocks. Last week, officials from the nuclear plant led a group of foreign journalists and aid workers on a tour of the disaster zone.

nuclear power plant or at the site of waste disposal. Such a release could be accidental, the result of equipment malfunction or human error. There is also the risk of an intentional release of nuclear radiation as an act of terrorism. Whether accidental or intentional, such a release could potentially destroy all biotic life in the affected area and make the area sterile for life for the foreseeable future.

Although as of [2003] there have been no intentional releases of nuclear radiation into the environment, there have been two serious accidents at nuclear power plants. In 1979, there was an accident at the Three Mile Island nuclear power plant in Pennsylvania. There was another accident in 1986 at the Chernobyl nuclear power plant in Ukraine. Although very little nuclear radiation escaped from the Three Mile Island accident, nuclear radiation did escape from the Chernobyl accident, causing substantial ecological damage and the deaths of a number of people.

SOURCE. *Richard O. Randolph, "Nuclear Energy,"* Encyclopedia of Science and Religion, *edited by J. Wentzel Vrede van Huyssteen, vol. 2. New York: Macmillan Reference USA, 2003.*

The concrete sarcophagus is to be covered by a new steel shell in 2008. Mrs Marusich said that debris stacked against the inside of the existing shell's southern wall is slowly shifting and "could result in the entire structure collapsing". Parts of the concrete shell are criss-crossed by cracks.

As preparations for the new structure advance, several thousand employees are working to dismantle the plant's remaining reactors and process the leftover nuclear fuel. Each night they are taken by train to Slavutich, the town built outside the dead zone especially for workers.

Visiting the skeleton of the city that Slavutich replaced is the most poignant moment on the Chernobyl tour. Pripyat was a model town with elite apartments, shops, swimming pools and kindergartens. A day and a half after Reactor Four exploded, the entire population of the city was loaded on to buses and taken away.

"There was a forest nearby that turned red from radioactive dust," remembered Nikolai, a driver who was a traffic policeman overseeing the evacuation that day. "People begged us to get past it as fast as we could."

Today, Pripyat is a ghost town where time has stood still. A fairground ride, finished days before the disaster, is enveloped in weeds and contorted vines. Birdsong is clear in the total silence.

Many locals are surprisingly unconcerned by the legacy of Chernobyl. About 600 people have returned to live inside the dead zone. Maria Dika, 42, leaning from a balcony in Chernobyl town, said she had suffered no long-term ill effects after three months of treatment for acute radiation sickness. She was working as a security guard at Reactor Four on the night of the disaster.

"We're fine," she joked. "No health problems. The radiation has got used to us." Tatiana Khrushch, 66, agreed. "The air's clean, the water's lovely and the mushrooms are great," she said. "This is a fine place."

CHAPTER 3
Personal Narratives

A Control Room Worker Talks About the Accident and Life Afterwards

Vivienne Parry

Vivienne Parry is a British columnist and journalist, as well as the science editor for *Good Housekeeping* magazine and a former presenter on the BBC's science program *Tomorrow's World*. For the following viewpoint she spoke with Sasha Yuvchenko, an engineer-mechanic who was working in unit four of the Chernobyl facility at the time of the explosion and meltdown of that unit's reactor. Yuvchenko and his coworkers absorbed an enormous amount of radiation. Although Yuvchenko, a former athlete, survived with a terribly withered arm, most of his coworkers died within weeks, and one was vaporized on the spot. Nonetheless, Yuvchenko still believes that nuclear energy can be used safely, provided safety is "the number-one priority in all developments."

SOURCE. Vivienne Parry, "How I Survived Chernobyl," *The Guardian*, August 24, 2004. Copyright © 2004 Guardian Newspapers Limited. Reproduced by permission of the author.

On April 25 1986, 24-year-old Sasha Yuvchenko clocked on as usual for the night shift at the Chernobyl power plant in northern Ukraine. It was a beautiful evening, particularly warm and clear, and Yuvchenko, an engineer-mechanic, and his workmates were full of their plans for the upcoming May Day holidays. At home, his wife, Natasha, was still up with their fretful two-year-old, Kirill.

On that fateful night, the water pumps in the newly commissioned No. 4 reactor were being safety-tested. As the clock ticked past midnight, an argument was raging about the right power level at which to start the test. But what no one knew, thanks to years of error and cover up, was that there was a fatal flaw in the reactor design that made it unstable at low power levels. As power levels were lowered in preparation for the test, they dropped too low and the reactor ground to a halt. Meanwhile, unseen, a dangerous hot spot was building deep in the reactor.

> 'The thick concrete walls were bent like rubber. I thought war had broken out.'

To raise the power, the boron control rods were removed. It was like cocking a gun, and when, at 1:20 AM on April 26 1986, the test began and the turbines were turned off, the reactor was turned into a volcanic steam pressure cooker. Emergency shutdown procedures were started, but when the control rods were reinserted, their graphite tips caused the power levels to rise so dramatically that a portion of the reactor was destroyed. There were two explosions and the 500-tonne safety cap was blown off the reactor. It was the worst nuclear accident in history.

Rushing to Secure the Building

Yuvchenko, now 42, recalls what happened that terrible night. He is a bear of a man, 6ft 5in tall, and a former Soviet champion rower. You can't help but notice his left

> 'You don't feel anything at the time. . . . We had no idea there was so much radiation.'

arm, which is half the size of his right and shiny with scar tissue. His wife, Natasha, sits nervously on the edge of her seat.

"There was a heavy thud," he says. "A couple of seconds later, I felt a wave come through the room. The thick concrete walls were bent like rubber. I thought war had broken out. We started to look for Khodemchuk (his colleague) but he had been by the pumps and had been vaporised. Steam wrapped around everything; it was dark and there was a horrible hissing noise. There was no ceiling, only sky; a sky full of stars." A stream of ionising radiation was shooting starwards, like a laser beam. "I remember thinking how beautiful it was."

Yuvchenko went with a party of men to recon the damaged reactor hall. He stayed outside, propping the heavy reactor hall door open with his shoulder. The three men who went in all died within two weeks. "You don't feel anything at the time," he explains. "We had no idea there was so much radiation. We met a guy with a doseometer and the needle was just off the dial. But even then, we were still only thinking, 'Rats, this means the end of our careers in the nuclear industry.' We all thought, 'We've been exposed now, this has happened on our watch' and set about doing what we could. After about an hour, I started to vomit uncontrollably. My throat was very sore."

By 6am, he could no longer walk. He was taken to the local hospital. Still he had no idea of the huge hit of radiation he'd received. "We were thinking we might have had 20, perhaps 50 rem. But there was a man there who'd been involved in a nuclear accident in the submarine fleet, he said it was more serious than that. 'You don't vomit at 50,' he said."

At the hospital, they worked out (through measuring the fall in his white blood-cell count) that he'd received

Many workers at Chernobyl who survived the nuclear reactor's explosion suffered horrific scars. (Chuck Nacke/Time Life Pictures/Getty Images.)

410 rem—or as it's now since been styled, 4.1 Sv (one sievert is equal to 100 rem)—a measure of the absorbed dose of radiation per kilogram of body weight. Four sieverts is lethal for half of those affected.

Enormous Radiation Exposure

In the EU [European Union], the maximum dose of radiation to which the population near a nuclear power station should be exposed to is one millisievert (mSv) a year, and for nuclear workers, it is 20 mSv annually. The average radiation dose from natural and medical radiation is 2.5 mSv. The plant workers and firefighters at Chernobyl received 650 times their permitted yearly dose and more than 5,000 times the average annual dose.

> "It is a truly horrible way to die, burnt from within and without."

Yuvchenko was seen once by a nurse during this time but was interviewed three times by the KGB [Soviet intelligence]. Startling film taken by the KGB of the devastated reactor is shown in a new documentary, *Zero Hour: Disaster at Chernobyl*. Whoever took the film is likely to have died.

Yuvchenko was then shipped off to Moscow. No one told Natasha where he was. A rule of thumb is that vomiting that starts within half an hour of irradiation indicates a fatal dose. Of those transported with him, five died. Those who died quickly were lucky. It is a truly horrible way to die, burnt from within and without.

Some 128 people were sent to the specialised treatment centre in Moscow. When Yuvchenko arrived, his head was shaved, but within days all his body hair fell out anyway. By now all were experiencing the effects of radiation to their lungs, nose, ears and throats. For those with severe exposures, rubber-like mucus caused breathing problems, and herpes-like rashes formed massive crusts on lips and facial skin. Those who had started vomiting early were given bone-marrow transplants. Yuvchenko received the first of many transfusions.

Nobody knows quite how radiation produces its early effects of nausea and diarrhoea. When the vomiting subsides, there is a period of calm. There is seemingly trivial reddening of the skin at first, but, again after a period of calm, the skin develops weeping ulcerations over layers of dead tissue. Yuvchenko recalls pulling back the sheets, and there being a cloud of black dust—his dead skin. A slime of gamma and beta-emitting nuclides had covered all surfaces in the plant after the explosion, and where his body had touched the door—his left shoulder, hip and calf—their deadly radiation had gnawed away at his flesh, causing the death of tissue deep in his arm. It became grossly swollen and his skin turned violet black.

No Cure for Radiation Exposure

He had the first of many, many operations and skin grafts. For a while, he thought that his arm would be amputated. Those champion muscles were his saviour. "Mine are small," he laughs, "you should see my little brother's." His arm was to be in bandages for the next seven years. He was plagued by—and occasionally still has—outbreaks of skin ulceration. Microsurgery in Berlin, in which blood vessels were transferred from his leg to his irradiated arm, finally saw him on the road to recovery. His colleagues were not all as lucky. One who worked in the turbine hall and took 10 Sv survived a bone-marrow transplant and blindness only to die after a few months.

Death after acute radiation exposure usually comes from infection as the radiation destroys bone-marrow cells, causing a catastrophic drop in infection-fighting white blood cells. The body is overwhelmed, particularly where there is intense damage to skin and intestine. People assume that there is something that you can take to prevent radiation damage, as they do in *Star Trek*. Potassium iodate tablets, taken within hours of exposure, flood the thyroid, and make uptake of radioactive iodine less likely. But iodine is only one of the radionuclides. Supportive care and rigorous infection control is all the medical care there is.

Yuvchenko spent a year in hospital and a further two in rehab. He attributes his survival to his treatment in Moscow—and those muscles. He doesn't know whether he is infertile—although this is highly likely—but in any case, was advised not to have another child because of the risk that they, or their children, would develop leukaemia. Chromosomal damage over 4 Sv is severe. What of his prospects now, particularly of cancer?

"The doctors told me that if you've survived this, you shouldn't worry about anything else." Every year, he has two weeks of check-ups. "I always think they might find something." But he has remained well, as has his wife and son, a tribute to the extraordinary repair properties of DNA.

Psychological Recovery Is More Challenging

"It's the nerves that get you," says Natasha. For many years, people literally ran away from them, terrified of contamination. The fear of radiation and what could happen, may yet prove to be a bigger killer than radiation itself. There have been nearly 2,000 cases of thyroid cancer, mostly in children, but the predicted surge in other types of cancer has, according to the Unscear [United Nations Scientific Committee on the Effects of Atomic Radiations] 2000 report, not yet been seen. But there have been big increases in deaths from heart disease, alcoholism and suicide in Belarus and Ukraine.

Yuvchenko considers himself lucky, especially compared with those whose extraordinary heroism finally brought the incident under control. Yuvchenko has a generous pension; they had nothing. And asked what he now thinks of the future of civil nuclear power, his answer is emphatic, and perhaps surprising. "If one learns the lessons and keeps safety as the number-one priority in all developments, then it is safe."

A Liquidator's Experience at Chernobyl

Sergei B., interviewed by Mark Resnicoff

In 1986 "Sergei B." was a Soviet military reservist and trained chemist. He volunteered to work as a "liquidator," cleaning up the site of the Chernobyl disaster. Sergei B.'s account demonstrates the futility of estimating radiation exposure from Chernobyl. He also highlights the constant shortages that plagued the Soviet Union: shortages in safety equipment, shortages of qualified personnel, and even food shortages that led to some liquidators eating locally produced fruit and vegetables, despite knowing that these were likely to be dangerously radioactive. Like other scientists who directly experienced the Chernobyl disaster, Sergei B. continues to believe that nuclear energy can be used safely.

Mark Resnicoff is an editor for the English-language components of Pripyat.com, a Web site about the town nearest to Chernobyl, and a feature writer specializing in European affairs for Suite101.com. Resnicoff also runs the Chernobyl and eastern Europe Web site Chernobylee.com, where he originally published the interview from which the following viewpoint is excerpted.

During the summer of 1986, Sergei B. was a 30-year-old army reservist who volunteered to go to Chernobyl in late July as a participant in cleanup operations. Sergei worked as a liquidator at the Chernobyl Plant through early September, visiting the facility 23 times. He worked on "special projects" at the plant and made six trips to the roof of Reactor 3, where liquidators worked quickly to remove highly-contaminated rubble from the accident. . . .

> Ph.D. scientists were sort of 'untouchables.' But I volunteered anyway.

Mark Resnicoff: Where were you living/stationed at the time of the accident?
Sergei B.: My brigade was headquartered nearby the village named Oranoe.

Why did you volunteer to go to Chernobyl?
I felt that I possessed the necessary knowledge and skills to do the work required—I had my secondary (military) education as an officer-chemist. At that time, in 1986, Ph.D. scientists had "carte blanche"; they had a power to decline the draft call (army reserve). Around May-June of 1986 there was a massive call-on for mid-rank officer staff because of the high personnel rotation in early the "liquidation" campaign, and Ph.D. scientists were sort of "untouchables." But I volunteered anyway.

How old were you when you volunteered?
I was 30 years old.

What were you doing at the time?

I was a Lecturer/Scientist at the Institute of Chemical Technology, Dnepropetrovsk.

When you volunteered, did you have any idea how serious the situation was, and that you would be risking your life? If not, when did you realize the situation was really bad?

As probably all of us liquidators, I did not have a clue what was going on until I'd got there. Even after the first couple of weeks it was hard to get a real picture, a grasp on the scale of operations and money tossed in the fix-up efforts. Only sometime in early August I realized that this is far beyond a one country problem—it is global. . . . However, it wasn't a feeling of the doomsday, it was an appreciation of what we are going to do, an understanding that it has to be done no matter what. Tremendous boost of the confidence. That helped to curtail the "I do risk my life here" precautionary sense.

> Doses accumulated by many of us during July-August-September of 1986 were artificially lowered in the paperwork.

Radiation Exposure Only Guessed At

You were in the Zone for just over one month. Was the short time frame due to your accumulated radiation exposure, or was it planned to be that length when you first arrived?

Yes, it was because I had accumulated the sacred number—25 Roentgens [R]. In reality my dose was at least trice [three times] higher (according to my estimates)—during my time in the Zone, we did not have individual dosimeters whatsoever; the dose was calculated based on the "average" working irradiation measurements, 6–8 check-points on the perimeter/mid-section of the operational field, surface, etc. Based on the "level," the squad leader such as myself determined the average time of work, considering daily dose of 2.5 Roentgens (not higher) per person.

By any chance, do you recall the highest radiation level you encountered? If so, do you recall the measurement and where it was?

The roof of the 3rd reactor building tops everything (figuratively)—levels of 1,500 R and higher were in a couple of spots on level "G," as far as I remember. However, on some Station grounds ("Object Pikatov," as they called contaminated soil scraped to the corner of the 3rd reactor) I once witnessed 1,200 R measurement. . . .

Do you recall the lowest radiation level you encountered? If so, what was the measurement and where was it?

Pretty much all the Station grounds around the main building—including the backyard behind it—were around 100 to 500 milliRoentgen at my times. The space was kept wet all the times, so it was an unbelievable swamp-like dirt layer in front of the main building, where Lenin's stela [statue] is.

I have read that the Soviet government kept liquidators in the Zone beyond what was considered safe limitations of radiation exposure. Do you feel that happened in your case, and if so, why?

Yes, it happened in my case and in many other cases—countless, actually—for several reasons. One was that there was not enough of individual dosimeters available during spring-summer of 1986 for everybody; only "civics," engineers and scientists, had them. We, "military," army reservists, did not. *Shortage* was a common word. Another reason was that it was not enough subs/rotation available, particularly of mid-rank officers, so doses accumulated by many of us during July-August-September of 1986 were artificially lowered in the paperwork.

On the other hand, the margins of "safe limitations" are still unknown. But this is a totally different subject.

Difficult Work in Dangerous Conditions

During your time in the Zone, you made 6 trips to the roof of Reactor 3. What did you do while on the roof? How long were you on the roof each time?

Time on the roof varied from as short as 45 sec. to as long as 3 min. depending on the current radiation level and place you have to work on. Sometimes, especially after the helicopter's treatment (they used special solutions to suppress the radiation/dust by dumping tons and tons of deactivating solution very early in the morning, before we started working there), levels were not as high, so we were able to work a bit longer. We chopped asphalt which contained pieces of highly radioactive solids sunk into molten asphalt on the explosion day (the asphalt solidified over them after the initial fire was put down) and tossed them down on the ground, over the roof edge. Last couple of raids I primarily guided my squad/troops simply because my cumulative dose was already too high and I was not "allowed" to accumulate more than 1.5 Roentgen per trip . . . which was a travesty anyway.

Can you describe the protective clothing you wore on the roof of Reactor 3? Was it easy to move around in it?

We had parts of the General Military Protective Kit (boots, gloves, head gear . . .), a heavy industrial respirator, and a unique "protective piece" of two thin (about 1/8–1/4 in.) rectangular lead plates, about 1.5 by 2.0 ft, covering front and back. They were tied together.

What type of work did you do during your other trips to the Chernobyl station?

> *After the first year people quickly forgot about who we are and what we did for them. . . . [They] became intolerant of our (liquidator's) benefits.*

I had to lead and to be responsible for a safe and efficient operation of a troop squad ranging from 10 to 25 soldiers (army reservists). The rotation of the troops was unbelievable: there was not a single day—and I had 15 trips/days in a row during one stretch in August—when I had more than 2–3 guys from the previous day with me. I barely remembered their names, forget faces—just because most of the time we were wearing masks/respirators, so it was really hard to recognize a person.

To answer shortly, I was involved in all major clean-up operations ranging from the roof of the 3rd reactor (highest radiation levels) to corridors of 1+2 reactor building clean-up (lowest, probably, at the time). We also had a task to build a barb-wire fence around the whole station at some point, just to increase a security level. Different story.

What was your pay as a liquidator? Were you paid extra due to the dangerous work environment?

Yes, I was paid after I got back, but strangely enough, it was a pay-off by my Institute, not by the government. Ukrainian Government picked up the tab of my pension—which wasn't that big after initial hefty paycheck after the USSR had collapsed (initial payment was about 5 times my monthly salary for those 3+ months I was in Chernobyl . . . this was specific extra pay for "dangerous environment work"). It was always a very pitiful feeling to go and get my pension. After the first year people quickly forgot about who we are and what we did for them. . . . [They] became intolerant of our (liquidator's) benefits. I have heard a lot of angry mumbling behind my back when I used a certificate—which I did quite seldom anyway. . . .

Ongoing Medical Issues

What did you do after leaving the Zone?

I had some health issues (heart, kidneys, etc.), which were somewhat contained, not because of the government help, but because of my connections/networking—I have several friends among prominent doctors back home, something which came out of my sports connection early on; I played a lot of semi-pro b[asket]-ball back in my 20's. . . .

So I was more or less fortunate to get straightened out without spending time in the hospital, and then continued to work at my Institute as Associate Professor. After the USSR collapsed, things went bad for my Institute, so I looked for a chance to get a post doc[toral] position in the US, which I got in 1992.

What type of medical issues have you dealt with since that time? Did you have to spend anytime in a hospital after leaving Chernobyl?

See above. I also was very careful and did not do stupid things like eating contaminated fruits and vegetables, as many of my fellow liquidators did in the Zone (see above about "shortage." . . . Many times I tried to warn them; some listened, some did not). But I still remember one of the physicians in my Brigade who said, "You guys (those who work on the Station) have to measure about 20 years from now for your dear life—that's all you've got!"

> I saw people fishing in a contaminated river, gathering and eating potatoes, mushrooms, etc.

How many of your friends that served as liquidators with you have become sick due to radiation exposure?

At least three of my fellow liquidators got health problems right there, while being involved at the Station. I know of several deaths among liquidators whom I served with, but this is a very sad and emotional part for me, so forgive me if I choose not to go into details.

While working as a liquidator, did you visit or work in Pripyat? If so, what were your impressions of this modern Soviet city?

Yes, I had a chance to go to Pripyat. It was an eerie experience—a true ghost city. Abandoned dogs (I haven't seen cats—I think they were eventually exterminated by stronger animals) were quite dangerous back then. I also had a chance to meet a few former station workers on the roads—they were scavenging their belongings from the city despite the government's ban. This was really heart-breaking.

My cousin worked on ChAES [Russian acronym for Chernobylski Atomica Elektrostabii; i.e., Chernobyl Atomic Power Plan] as an electrician; his younger son, my nephew, became very sick (they were staying home on that weekend . . . in Pripyat) and up until now he still cannot recover.

Abandoned Cities and Refugees

If you did spend time in Pripyat, since the city was evacuated, what kind of activities occurred in the city? Did some liquidators live in the apartments or hostels? What facilities were still usable (cultural center, pool, stadium, etc.)?

At the time I had visited Pripyat, there was no people allowed to live there, there was barb wire all around, and MPs [military police] were patrolling the empty roads on BTRs [armored personnel carriers]; if I remember correctly, it was around mid-August, but I might be wrong.

Did you have many (or any) interactions with people who lived in the town of Chernobyl or one of the villages in the area? If so, what were their concerns? Were they scared?

Many still did not believe that radiation is an imminent threat. I saw people fishing in a contaminated river, gathering and eating potatoes, mushrooms, etc. Whoever was scared, fled the area way too fast. Who's left, were just sad and very upset with the absence of help—on any level. Locals called the accident "the war." . . .

Do you remember anything about the village Kopachi? Was there any reason to believe the military would eventually bulldoze all the wooden buildings and bury them? Did the area seem to be that contaminated?

I am not really aware of this story. But once again I will ask about definition of "being that contaminated." The whole Zone—and far beyond it—resembled a cheetah skin, where dark spots were small contamination areas. One of them was probably in Kopachi village.

I remember a place in a remote railway station, where an abandoned rail car, which stood on the backtrack for several weeks, had a single spot on the wooden side blazing about 15–20 Roentgens consistently. My friends, dosimetrists had to check their dosimeters on it. . . .

How do you feel about the looters and marauders that have caused damage in Pripyat and some of the villages? What about their removing items from the Exclusion Zone and selling them to unsuspecting people?

This is, sadly, one of the expected outcomes of the whole isolation process. Again think of the word "shortage"—if not that, people probably would think twice before buying anything second-hand at such time as a nuclear accident, even far away from that place. . . .

Before going there, I remember we were carefully checking license plates of trucks selling potatoes on local veggie markets—if they were from Kiev District, we were avoiding them.

> I think people back home made it a Barnum circus . . . I know that many guys tried to make a living out of their Chernobyl times.

Abandoning Ukraine

During the time you worked as a liquidator, what were your feelings toward the Soviet government? What are your feelings toward the Soviet government today?

I still think that the cover-up was absolutely uncalled for. But again, Chernobyl together with some other events brought the country down. So the government was afraid for a reason, although I totally hated it then and still do hate it. Propaganda was a lifestyle in that country.

When did you move to the United States and why?

I moved to the US in late 1992. I realized that there is no life for me in the new country which did not care about education and/or science—it was purely survival mode for "new Ukraine." I did not want to end up on the street, as some of my teacher friends did.

I had a good chance to get in the US as a researcher. I used it. I hope I served my new country well ever since. . . .

Since you now live in the US, do you receive a liquidator's pension?

No.

Have you been back to Chernobyl since your tour of duty?

No, I have not. I actually do not want to. I think people back home made it a Barnum circus; I do not like that. I know that many guys tried to make a living out of their Chernobyl times, either career in the governmental organizations or in various Unions, Assemblies, etc. I know that the guy who came to substitute for me now became a District Chairman for Chernobyl Veteran Organization. He claimed to do things in the Zone which I know for sure he never did. . . . He's got medals, honorary addresses, high pension, etc. . . . That's pretty pitiful.

Considering your experiences at Chernobyl, are you for or against nuclear power? What are your feelings regarding nuclear power?

As a scientist, I know for sure that mankind has no alternative for nuclear power. It's clean, very efficient, and safe (well, except cases when people just violate rules and common sense . . .).

Women and Children in Chernobyl

Svetlana Alexievich

Svetlana Alexievich is an awarded-winning Belarusian journalist and essayist. She is most noted for her narrative accounts of important world events; these are based on many hours of interviews she conducts with eyewitnesses and often focus on the experiences of women and children. The following viewpoint is drawn from her book *Voices from Chernobyl: The Oral History of a Nuclear Disaster*. These selections recount the experiences of the wives and children of liquidators and plant workers living in Pripyat. Less than two miles from the Chernobyl plant, this city of fifty thousand was built specifically to house the facility's staff and their families and had to be entirely abandoned following the accident.

The viewpoint combines several accounts, including those of the mother of a girl born terribly deformed after the accident; a Pripyat housewife's recollection of her family's displacement

SOURCE. Svetlana Alexievich, *Voices from Chernobyl: The Oral History of a Nuclear Disaster*. Normal, IL: Dalkey Archive Press, 2005. Copyright © 1997, 2006 by Svetlana Alexievich. Preface and translation copyright © by Keith Gessen. All rights reserved. Reproduced by permission.

following the disaster; and snippets of children's memories of the accident, evacuation, and aftermath.

Lovisa Z., Mother

My little daughter—she's different. She's not like the others. She's going to grow up and ask me: "Why aren't I like the others?"

When she was born, she wasn't a baby, she was a little sack, sewed up everywhere, not a single opening, just the eyes. The medical card says: "Girl, born with multiple complex pathologies: aplasia of the anus, aplasia of the vagina, aplasia of the left kidney." That's how it sounds in medical talk, but more simply: no pee-pee, no butt, one kidney. On the second day I watched her get operated on, on the second day of her life. She opened her eyes and smiled, and I thought that she was about to start crying. But, God, she smiled!

The ones like her don't live, they die right away. But she didn't die, because I loved her.

In four years she's had four operations. She's the only child in Belarus to have survived being born with such complex pathologies. I love her so much. [*Stops.*] I won't be able to give birth again. I wouldn't dare. I came back from the maternity ward, my husband would start kissing me at night, I would lie there and tremble: we can't, it's a sin, I'm scared. I heard the doctors talking: "That girl wasn't born in a shirt, she was born in a suit of armor. If we showed it on television, not a single mother would give birth." That was about our daughter. How are we supposed to love each other after that?

I went to church and told the minister. He said I needed to pray for my sins. But no one in my family ever killed anyone. What am I guilty of? First they wanted to evacuate our village, and then they crossed it off their lists—the government didn't have enough money. And

> I'm all right with her becoming a lab frog, a lab rabbit, just as long as she lives.

right around then I fell in love. I got married. I didn't know that we weren't allowed to love here. Many years ago, my grandmother read in the Bible that there will be a time when everything is thriving, everything blossoming and fruitful, and there will be many fish in the rivers and animals in the forest, but man won't be able to use any of it. And he won't be able to propagate himself in his likeness, to continue his line. I listened to the old prophecies like they were scary fairy tales. I didn't believe them.

Tell everyone about my daughter. Write it down. She's four years old and she can sing, dance, she knows poetry by heart. Her mental development is normal, she isn't any different from the other kids, only her games are different. She doesn't play "store," or "school"—she plays "hospital." She gives her dolls shots, takes their temperature, puts them on IV. If a doll dies, she covers it with a white sheet. We've been living in the hospital with her for four years, we can't leave her there alone, and she doesn't even know that you're supposed to live at home. When we go home for a month or two, she asks me, "When are we going back to the hospital?" That's where her friends are, that's where they're growing up.

They made an anus for her. And they're forming a vagina. After the last operation her urinary functioning completely broke down, and they were unable to insert a catheter—they'll need more operations for that. But from here on out they've advised us to seek medical help abroad. Where are we going to get tens of thousands of dollars if my husband makes 120 dollars a month? One professor told us quietly: "With her pathologies, your child is of great interest to science. You should write to hospitals in other countries. They would be interested." So I write. [*Tries not to cry.*] I write that every half hour we have to squeeze out her urine manually, it comes out through artificial openings in the area of her vagina. Where else is there a child in the world who has to have her urine squeezed out of her every half hour? And how much longer can it go on? No one knows the effect of small doses of radiation on the organism of a child. Take my girl, even if it's to experiment. I don't want her to die! I'm all right with her becoming a lab frog, a lab rabbit, just as long as she lives. [*Cries.*] I've written dozens of letters. Oh, God!

She doesn't understand yet, but someday she'll ask us: why isn't she like everyone else? Why can't she love a man? Why can't she have babies? Why won't what happens to butter- flies ever happen to her? What hap- pens to birds? To everyone but her? I wanted—I should have been able to prove—so that—I wanted to get papers—so that she'd know—when she grew up—it wasn't our fault, my husband and I, it wasn't our love that was at fault. [*Tries again not to cry.*] I fought for four

> "The doctors said: 'We have instructions. We are supposed to call incidents of this type general sicknesses.'"

years—with the doctors, the bureaucrats—I knocked on the doors of important people. It took me four years to finally get a paper from the doctors that confirmed the connection between ionized radiation (in small doses) and her terrible condition. They refused me for four years; they kept telling me: "Your child is a victim of a congenital handicap." What congenital handicap? She's a victim of Chernobyl! I studied my family tree—nothing like this has ever happened in our family. Everyone lived until they were eighty or ninety. My grandfather lived until he was 94. The doctors said: "We have instructions. We are supposed to call incidents of this type general sicknesses. In twenty or thirty years, when we have a database about Chernobyl, we'll begin connecting these to ionized radiation. But for the moment science doesn't know enough about it." But I can't wait twenty or thirty years. I wanted to sue them. Sue the government. They called me crazy, laughed at me, like, there were children like these in ancient Greece, too. One bureaucrat yelled at me: "You want Chernobyl privileges! Chernobyl victim funds!" How I didn't faint in his office, I'll never know.

There was one thing they didn't understand—didn't want to understand—I needed to know that it wasn't our fault. It wasn't our love. [*Breaks down. Cries.*] This girl is growing up—she's still a girl—I don't want you to print our name—even our neighbors—even other people on our floor don't know. I'll put a dress on her, and a handkerchief, and they say, "Your Katya is so pretty." Meanwhile I give pregnant women the strangest looks. I don't look at them, I kind of glance at them real quick. I have all these mixed feelings: surprise and horror, jealousy and joy, even this feeling of vengeance. One time I caught myself thinking that I look the same way at the neighbors' pregnant dog—at the bird in its nest. . . .

Nadezhda Vygovskaya, Evacuee From the Town of Pripyat

At first the question was, Who's to blame? But then, when we learned more, we started thinking, What should we do? How do we save ourselves? After realizing that this would not be for one year or for two, but for many generations, we began to look back, turning the pages.

It happened late Friday night. That morning no one suspected anything. I sent my son to school, my husband went to the barber's. I'm preparing lunch when my husband comes back. "There's some sort of fire at the nuclear plant," he says. "They're saying we are not to turn off the radio." I forgot to say that we lived in Pripyat, near the reactor. I can still see the bright-crimson glow, it was like the reactor was glowing. This wasn't any ordinary fire, it was some kind of emanation. It was pretty. I'd

> At eight that morning, there were already military people on the streets in gas masks.

never seen anything like it in the movies. That evening everyone spilled out onto their balconies, and those who didn't have them went to friends' houses. We were on the ninth floor, we had a great view. People brought their kids out, picked them up, said, "Look! Remember!" And these were people who worked at the reactor—engineers, workers, physics instructors. They stood in the black dust, talking, breathing, wondering at it. People came from all around on their cars and their bikes to have a look. We didn't know that death could be so beautiful. Though I wouldn't say that it had no smell—it wasn't a spring or an autumn smell, but something else, and it wasn't the smell of earth. My throat tickled, and my eyes watered.

I didn't sleep all night, and I heard the neighbors walking around upstairs, also not sleeping. They were carrying stuff around, banging things, maybe they were packing their belongings. I fought off my headache with Citramon tablets [similar to aspirin]. In the morning I woke up and looked around and I remember feeling— this isn't something I made up later, I thought it right then—something isn't right, something has changed forever. At eight that morning, there were already military people on the streets in gas masks. When we saw them on the streets, with all the military vehicles, we didn't grow frightened—on the contrary, it calmed us. The army is here, everything will be fine. We didn't understand then that the "peaceful atom" could kill, that man is helpless before the laws of physics.

> I often dream that I'm riding through sunny Pripyat with my son. It's a ghost town now. But we're riding through and looking at the roses.

All day on the radio they were telling people to prepare for an evacuation: they'd take us away for three days, wash everything, check things out. The kids were told to take their school books. Still, my husband put our documents and our wedding photos in his briefcase. The only thing I took was a gauze kerchief in case the weather turned bad.

> **The puddles were yellow and green, like someone had poured paint into them. They said it was dust from the flowers.**

From the very first I felt that we were Chernobylites, that we were already a separate people. Our bus stopped overnight in a village; people slept on the floor in a school, others in a club. There was nowhere to go. One woman invited us to sleep at her house. "Come," she said, "I'll put down some linen for you. I feel bad for your boy." Her friend started dragging her away from us. "Are you crazy? They're contaminated!" When we settled in Mogilev and our son started school, he came back the very first day in tears. They put him next to a girl who said she didn't want to sit with him, he was radioactive. Our son was in the fourth grade, and he was the only one from Chernobyl in the class. The other kids were afraid of him, they called him "Shiny." His childhood ended so early.

As we were leaving Pripyat there was an army column heading back in the other direction. There were so many military vehicles—that's when I grew frightened. But I couldn't shake the feeling that this was all happening to someone else. I was crying, looking for food, sleeping, hugging my son, calming him down, but inside, this constant sense that I was just an observer. In Kiev they gave us some money, but we couldn't buy anything: hundreds of thousands of people had been uprooted and they'd bought everything up and eaten everything. Many had heart attacks and strokes, right there at the train stations, on the buses. I was saved by my mother. She'd lived a long time and had lost everything more than once. The first time was in the 1930s, they took her cow, her horse, her house. The second time, there'd been a fire, the only thing she'd saved was me. Now she said, "We have to get through it. After all, we're alive."

I remember one thing: we're on the bus, everyone's crying. A man up front is yelling at his wife. "I can't believe you'd be so stupid! Everyone else brought their things, and all we've got are these three-liter bottles!" The wife had decided that since they were taking the bus, she might as well bring some empty pickling bottles for her mother, who was on the way. They had these big bulging sacks next to their seats, we kept tripping over them the whole way to Kiev, and that's what they came to Kiev with.

Now I sing in the church choir. I read the Bible. I go to church—it's the only place they talk about eternal life. They comfort a person. You won't hear those words anywhere else, and you so want to hear them.

I often dream that I'm riding through sunny Pripyat with my son. It's a ghost town now. But we're riding through and looking at the roses, there were many roses in Pripyat, large bushes with roses. I was young. My son was little. I loved him. And in the dream I've forgotten all the fears, as if I were just a spectator the whole time.

Children's Memories of Chernobyl

There was a black cloud, and hard rain. The puddles were yellow and green, like someone had poured paint into them. They said it was dust from the flowers. Grandma made us stay in the cellar. She got down on her knees and prayed. And she taught us, too. "Pray! It's the end of the world. It's God's punishment for our sins." My brother was eight and I was six. We started remembering our sins. He broke the glass can with the raspberry jam, and I didn't tell my mom that I got my new dress caught on a fence and it ripped. I hid it in the closet.

*

Soldiers came for us in cars. I thought the war had started. They were saying these things: "deactivation,"

> The sparrows disappeared from our town in the first year after the accident. They were lying around everywhere—in the yards, on the asphalt.

"isotopes." One soldier was chasing after a cat. The dosimeter was working on the cat like an automatic [weapon]: click, click. A boy and a girl were chasing the cat, too. The boy was all right, but the girl kept crying, "I won't give him up!" She was yelling: "Run away, run little girl!" But the soldier had a big plastic bag.

*

I heard—the adults were talking—Grandma was crying—since the year I was born [1986], there haven't been any boys or girls born in our village. I'm the only one. The doctors said I couldn't be born. But my mom ran away from the hospital and hid at Grandma's. So I was born at Grandma's. I heard them talking about it.

I don't have a brother or sister. I want one.

Tell me, lady, how could it be that I wouldn't be born? Where would I be? High in the sky? On another planet?

*

The sparrows disappeared from our town in the first year after the accident. They were lying around everywhere—in the yards, on the asphalt. They'd be raked up and taken away in the containers with the leaves. People weren't allowed to burn the leaves that year, because they were radioactive, so they buried the leaves.

The sparrows came back two years later. We were so happy, we yelled to each other: "I saw a sparrow yesterday! They're back."

The May bugs also disappeared, and they haven't come back. Maybe they'll come back in a hundred years or a thousand. That's what our teacher says. I won't see them.

*

September first, the first day of school, and there wasn't a single flower. The flowers were radioactive. Before the beginning of the year, the people working weren't masons, like before, but soldiers. They mowed the flowers, took off the earth and took it away somewhere in cars with trailers.

In a year they evacuated all of us and buried the village. My father's a cab driver, he drove there and told us about it. First they'd tear a big pit in the ground, five meters deep. Then the firemen would come up and use their hoses to wash the house from its roof to its foundation, so that no radioactive dust got kicked up. They wash the windows, the roof, the door, all of it. Then a crane drags the house from its spot and puts it down into the pit. There's dolls and books and cans all scattered around. The excavator picks them up. Then it covers everything with sand and clay, leveling it. And then instead of a village, you have an empty field. They sowed our land with corn. Our house is lying there, and our school and our village council office. My plants are there and two albums of stamps, I was hoping to bring them with me. Also I had a bike.

> They worked pretty close to the reactor. It was quiet and peaceful and pretty.

*

I'm twelve years old and I'm an invalid. The mailman brings two pension checks to our house—for me and my granddad. When the girls in my class found out that I had cancer of the blood, they were afraid to sit next to me. They didn't want to touch me.

The doctors said that I got sick because my father worked at Chernobyl. And after that I was born. I love my father.

Residents of Pripyat, Ukraine, were told after the Chernobyl accident that they were being evacuated for only three days. Little did they know the evacuation would be permanent. (Scott Peterson/Liason/Getty Images.)

*

They came for my father at night. I didn't hear how he got packed, I was asleep. In the morning I saw my mother was crying. She said, "Papa's in Chernobyl now."

We waited for him like he was at the war.

He came back and started going to the factory again. He didn't tell us anything. At school I bragged to everyone that my father just came back from Chernobyl, that he was a liquidator, and the liquidators were the ones who helped clean up after the accident. They were heroes. All the boys were jealous.

A year later he got sick.

We walked around in the hospital courtyard—this was after his second operation—and that was the first time he told me about Chernobyl.

They worked pretty close to the reactor. It was quiet and peaceful and pretty, he said. They took off the topsoil contaminated by cesium and strontium, and they washed the roofs. The next day everything would be "clicking" on the dosimeters again.

"In parting they shook our hands and gave us certificates of gratitude for our self-sacrifice." He talked and talked. The last time he came back from the hospital, he said: "If I stay alive, no more physics or chemistry for me. I'll leave the factory. I'll become a shepherd." My mom and I are alone now. I won't go to the technical institute, even though she wants me to. That's where my dad went.

*

I used to write poems. I was in love with a girl. In fifth grade. In seventh grade I found out about death.

I had a friend, Andrei. They did two operations on him and then sent him home. Six months later he was supposed to get a third operation. He hanged himself from his belt, in an empty classroom, when everyone else had gone to gym glass. The doctors had said he wasn't allowed to run or jump.

Yulia, Katya, Vadim, Oksana, Oleg, and now Andrei. "We'll die, and then we'll become science," Andrei used to say. "We'll die and everyone will forget us," Katya said. "When I die, don't bury me at the cemetery, I'm afraid of the cemetery, there are only dead people and crows there," said Oksana. "Bury me in the field." Yulia used to just cry. The whole sky is alive for me now when I look at it, because they're all there.

Poems by a Pripyat Refugee

Lyubov Sirota, translated by Leonid Levin and Elisavietta Ritchie

> Lyubov Sirota is a poet now living in Kiev, the capital of Ukraine. At the time of the Chernobyl accident, Sirota was living with her young son in the Pripyat neighborhood closest to the reactor. Early on the morning of April 26, 1986, Sirota could not sleep. She stepped out on her balcony to get some fresh air, and was among the few residents of Pripyat to actually witness the explosion of reactor number 4. Thirty-six hours later she, and every other resident of the city, was evacuated, leaving all of their belongings behind to rot and crumble. Soviet news media did not report on Pripyat for the next two months. In the following poems Sirota gives voice to the outrage and despair common among Chernobyl refugees, who feel ostracized in their new communities and ignored by their government.

SOURCE. Lyubov Sirota, "They Did Not Register Us (To Vasily Deomidovich Dubodel, who passed away 1988, and to all past and future victims of Chernobyl) and Radiophobia," *Chernobyl Poems by Lyubov Sirota*, November 11, 2003, translated by Leonid Levin and Elisavietta Ritchie. Reproduced by permission of the author's US agent.

"They Did Not Register Us"

(To Vasily Deomidovich Dubodel, who passed away in August 1988, and to all past and future victims of Chernobyl.)

They did not register us
and our deaths
were not linked to the accident.
No processions laid wreaths,
no brass bands melted with grief.
They wrote us off as
lingering stress,
cunning genetic disorders . . .
But we—we are the payment for rapid progress,
mere victim of someone else's sated afternoons.
It wouldn't have been so annoying for us to die
had we known
our death would help
to avoid more "fatal mistakes"
and halt replication of "reckless deeds"!
But thousands of "competent" functionaries
count our "souls" in percentages,
their own honesty, souls, long gone—
so we suffocate with despair.
They wrote us off.
They keep trying to write off
our ailing truths
with their sanctimonious lies.
But nothing will silence us!
Even after death,
from our graves
we will appeal to your Conscience
not to transform the Earth
into a sarcophagus!

* * *

Peace unto your remains,
unknown fellow-villager!
We'll all end up there sooner or later.
Like everyone, you wanted to live.
As it turned out,
you could not survive . . .

Your torment is done.
Our turn will come:
prepare us a roomier place over there.
Oh, if only our "mass departure"
could be a burning lump of truth
in duplicity's throat! . . .

May God not let anyone else
know our anguish!
May we be extinction's limit.
For this, you died.
Peace unto your remains,
my fellow-villager
from abandoned hamlets.

Radiophobia

Is this only—a fear of radiation?
Perhaps rather—a fear of wars?
Perhaps—the dread of betrayal,
cowardice, stupidity, lawlessness?
The time has come to sort out
what is—radiophobia.
It is—
when those who've gone through the Chernobyl
  drama
refuse to submit
to the truth meted out by government ministers
("Here, you swallow exactly this much today!")
We will not be resigned
to falsified ciphers,

base thoughts,
however you brand us!
We don't wish—and don't you suggest it!—
to view the world through bureaucratic glasses!
We're too suspicious!
And, understand, we remember
each victim just like a brother! . . .
Now we look out at a fragile Earth
through the panes of abandoned buildings.
These glasses no longer deceive us!—
These glasses show us more clearly—
believe me—
the shrinking rivers,
poisoned forests,
children born not to survive . . .
Mighty uncles, what have you dished out
beyond bravado on television?

Tens of thousands who lived in Pripyat until the nuclear disaster were evacuated within 36 hours of the event, never to return home. (Sergei Supinsky/ AFP/Getty Images.)

How marvelously the children have absorbed
radiation, once believed so hazardous! . . .
(It's adults who suffer radiophobia—
for kids is it still adaptation?)
What has become of the world
if the most humane of professions
has also turned bureaucratic?
Radiophobia
may you be omnipresent!
Not waiting until additional jolts,
new tragedies,
have transformed more thousands
who survived the inferno
into seers—
Radiophobia might cure
the world
of carelessness, satiety, greed,
bureaucratism and lack of spirituality,
so that we don't, through someone's good will
mutate into non-humankind.

An Irish Activist Working with "Chernobyl Orphans"

Adi Roche

Adi Roche is founder of Chernobyl Children's Project International (www.chernobyl-international.org), an organization that helps families and communities in Belarus and Ukraine who are affected by the Chernobyl disaster. CCPI supports life saving children's cardiac operations, nursing and therapeutic care and training programs, programs that take children out of orphanages and place them in homes, at home care for disabled children, community centers, humanitarian aid, and more. The largely volunteer organization was established in 1991.

When the accident at Chernobyl happened in 1986, Irish CND [Campaign for Nuclear Disarmament], in conjunction with the Irish Medical Campaign for the Prevention of Nuclear War,

---

SOURCE. Adi Roche, "A Personal Journey," from *Chernobyl Heart*, Copyright © 2008 by Adi Roche, Chernobyl Children's Project International. Reproduced by permission.

> The look of expectation in that child's face was enough to shatter my heart.

provided a 24-hour information hotline giving basic help and support to the general public, who were deeply concerned about the safety not only of themselves but, more specifically, for the well-being of their children. Our medical team was led by two Cork-based doctors, Mary and Seán Dunphy, who provided useful information regarding simple precautions parents could take to keep their children safe.

After the initial emergency receded, there was little or no information about the scale or consequences of the accident during the following few years. Every so often there was the odd article in some papers, but nothing that caught the imagination or interest of the general public. The word 'Chernobyl' disappeared from practically everyone's consciousness. I continued to include the issue in my Peace Education Programme and tried to learn as much as I could regarding the aftermath of the calamity. It wasn't until January 1991 that I received a fax message which broke through the earlier years of silence and sparse information. I will never forget the message because it was to have a major impact not only on the direction of my work with CND, but on the rest of my life. The message was simple and to the point: 'SOS Appeal. For God's sake help us to get the children out.' The fax originated from Belarusian and Ukrainian doctors, begging that the children of Chernobyl be taken away from their radioactive environment so that their bodies had some chance of recovery. The fax was our first breakthrough. Our response was immediate, with the first group of Chernobyl children arriving in Ireland for rest and recuperation in the summer of 1991. The children touched us deeply with their beauty, effervescence, love and friendship. It's one thing to know and understand what radioactivity does to human beings, but meeting, seeing and getting to know and love the child victims of radiation is another story altogether. Up to that point I was able to intellectualise the effects of radiation, and could reel off the facts and figures about nuclear power and nuclear weapons. It wasn't until I started working with the children and their communities that I fully realised the dark tragedy that had unfolded itself into the lives of those affected. What I knew in my head I could now translate into something real in my heart.

The day I received the faxed SOS appeal, I was working with my great friend and colleague Norrie McGregor, and together we started to work on trying to do something for the children of Chernobyl. Eventually both of us, with another great friend, Mary Aherne, decided that this was where we wanted to focus our work. We eventually formed a new organisation and called it The Chernobyl Children's Project International, an organisation that would work exclusively on the issue of Chernobyl. Later that year Mary Aherne, Mary Murray and I became the first Irish women to visit the Chernobyl region. Our first trip proved to be a harrowing one. The authorities controlled every aspect of our visit, but we still managed to get an understanding of the situation. I remember visiting a place where children had been abandoned at birth by parents who were unable to cope with their babies' deformities or retardations. Seeing the pain of the babies and children suffering without the help of painkillers and basic medicines was almost unbearable. We saw babies with no mental capacity and babies in permanent pain with distorted and broken bodies. They were oblivious to life around them, locked inside their tormented shapes, awaiting death. We saw children without limbs, a little girl who was so badly contorted that her legs grew up towards her body, youngsters with cruel mental handicaps and others with huge growths on their heads and bodies. The doctors and nurses, who loved their patients, could do little, since they lacked even the most basic medicines and equipment. Mothers and doctors alike made no secret of the fact that if they had had the equipment to identify the foetal defects in the womb, they would not have allowed these children to have been brought into the world.

In Minsk, Belarus I held a little boy called Uri in my arms and literally felt his life draining away from him. His face and his shrunken body will be one of the memories I will always carry with me. He died shortly after we left. He was suffering from hydrocephaly, a condition where fluid builds up around the brain. All that is required to alleviate the pressure that builds up on the brain is a mere 20-minute surgical procedure, called a shunt, which costs $200. But neither the money nor the simple procedure were available. The overwhelming memory I have of visiting this place in Minsk is the sound of Uri's crying, the doctors' crying and our own. We visited many hospitals, orphanages and communities and each had a story to tell. Visiting orphanages was the most difficult thing to do. It wasn't that these children weren't loved; their parents were no longer capable of dealing with the scale and impact that Chernobyl had had on their lives. These places were full of little boys and girls bursting to be loved and cuddled. They danced and sang their hearts out in order to entertain these three Irish women who had come bringing toys, food and clothing. We were the first foreigners the children had ever seen. My breaking point was when a little girl in one orphanage tugged the corner of my skirt and drew me to the door, crying 'Mamma, Mamma.' The look of expectation in that child's face was enough to shatter my heart.

The impact of this first visit proved to be a catalyst for action, along with the memories of all the children we had met in the institutions and orphanages, the medics and parents. Conditions in most orphan-

> What made it bearable was meeting the children who had been to Ireland and seeing the clear effects of their rest and recuperation in the country.

ages were the same—cold, smelly and sparsely furnished. We discovered that in winter they often had little or no heating, despite the severity of their weather. Their diets were also poor nutritionally, so many of the children could not fight off even the mildest infection or cold.

What made it bearable was meeting the children who had been to Ireland and seeing the clear effects of their rest and recuperation in the country. The children who had been with us were faring much better during the severe winter and suffered less illness, since their 'Irish families' had supplied them with multivitamins and tonics.

I remember speaking to Dr Emma in one of the orphanages. She showed us a medicine cabinet which contained only three small bottles of medicine, with no prospect of replacing even those, let alone obtaining sufficient supplies for all the children. There were two radioactive 'hot spots' near the orphanage and the doctor was fearful for the children's health. She herself felt unwell, but said she was afraid to die because then there would be no one to look after the children. Her sorrow was etched in her face. Dr Emma spoke about her personal memory of the accident: 'It was a strange smell, a taste in the mouth and back of the throat, like something metallic was there in the air. I knew nothing about the accident then. I just knew something had changed. It wasn't until I heard it on Freedom Radio [a US funded radio station transmitted from Western Europe to the former USSR] but I thought it was typical Western propaganda! But in this case it was the truth. I gave a small dose of iodine to my family. I didn't have it for the others in my care. I am sorry, so sorry about that. Many of them now have thyroid cancer. But what else was I to do?'

All we could do was to tell her truthfully that we would do everything in our power to assist them, and from that moment I began to plan a variety of ways to give support. Since that time, I have returned to the zones over 40 times. Each time there has been a purpose, either to deliver aid, bring sick children back to Ireland for treatment, to film documentaries highlighting their plight, to organize building projects or to set up medical health care programmes. Every time I return to the heart of the Chernobyl zone in Belarus, I witness a country on its knees, struggling to fight against the invisible enemy of radiation, an enemy that is slowly destroying its people. Through the people we have met over the past 20 years, both victims and those working to help the victims, we have seen the true cost of Chernobyl and can only speculate as to what the future holds for the people of the region. We travelled deep into the radiation zones, delivering aid and talking to the survivors. We measured frighteningly high levels of radioactivity. Scientists working in the area told how the zone is expanding, not contracting as expected, by about 10 km each year, eating into the land around it. One scientist, Professor Vasily Nesterenko, told us that 'it is impossible to say whether we are over the peak of the consequences of radioactive contamination or whether we are just on the threshold.' What a tragedy. It's a stain on human history. Like so many other countries on the tank paths of World War II, Belarusians suffered desperate atrocities at the hands of the Nazis during the war. They suffered again during Stalin's reign, and then came Chernobyl. Unlike war and its ravages, unlike hunger and disease, radioactive contamination poisoning will never leave Belarus and the other Chernobyl-affected regions. I wonder what future generations will think about what we have done to this beautiful earth. Unless our descendants come up with a way to neutralise the mountains of nuclear waste and contamination, they will condemn us as irresponsible nuclear joy riders who attempted to ride a wild beast bare backed, halterless and blindfolded.

A Chernobyl Tourist

Charles Hawley

Charles Hawley is a journalist and editor for *Spiegel Online*, Germany's most popular online news source. *Spiegel Online* is the sister edition to the weekly print magazine *Der Spiegel*, which has the largest circulation of any weekly magazine in Europe.

In the following viewpoint, Hawley describes what it is like to take a day trip into the radioactive exclusion zone surrounding Chernobyl. Many tourists come to snap photos of the crumbling steel-and-cement sarcophagus surrounding the remains of reactor unit number four, as well as Pripyat's abandoned May Day decorations—including decaying carnival attractions and the rusting skeleton of a Ferris wheel. What is perhaps most remarkable is the degree to which the radioactive area within the exclusion zone, largely free of human development, has become a wildlife preserve and refuge.

Tree branches on both sides of the desolate, two-lane road hang low with melting slush as we approach the Chernobyl exclusion zone in northern Ukraine on an unseasonably non-frigid late December

---

day in 2003. Heavy, gray clouds press down on the damp, white landscape. Cars are nowhere to be seen, freeing our rickety old Skoda station wagon to swerve away from the deepest of the plentiful potholes.

Before long, a small, wooden hut comes into view with a metal gate blocking further progress. A guard emerges, checks my driver's papers, checks my permit allowing me into the zone, raises the gate and we are in—free to explore the site of the worst civilian nuclear disaster ever to befall mankind.

> "A sign indicates we are entering a village, but not a house is to be seen."

Just past the entrance, a sign indicates we are entering a village, but not a house is to be seen. The forest, just as before, presses right up to the shoulder of the highway. The driver slows down and then points to the right and left. There, nestled into the forest, are the soggy, snow-covered farmhouses of an abandoned village. Save for the trees that have grown wildly for 20 years and rooted their way into the foundations, the village looks as though it could have been abandoned yesterday. An elk wanders across the road in front of us.

Just after midnight on April 26, 1986, reactor No. 4 at the Chernobyl nuclear power plant, located on the Prypiat River some 130 kilometers north of Kiev, exploded. The meltdown and ensuing fire spewed vast quantities of deadly radiation into the atmosphere—and it spread swiftly. Nearby forests quickly died, fields and orchards became unusable as the soil sucked up radiation, particularly beneath the numerous spring showers that fell from irradiated clouds that day. The invisible cloud of radiation eventually spread across the Soviet Union, Central Europe, Scandinavia and beyond.

An Image of Decay

While the rest of the world clamoured for information from the reticent Soviet authorities, a massive, emergency evacuation got underway in the villages, towns and cities near the stricken reactor. Buses pulled up to the entrances of the concrete block apartments in Prypiat—a purpose-built industrial city for Chernobyl workers with a pre-disaster population of almost 50,000—and ordered people to board. Some 12,500 were evacuated from the centuries-old town of Chernobyl and a further 100,000 had to abandon their family homes, property and belongings in villages located within the hastily established exclusion zone, radiating 30 kilometers (18.6 miles)—an area of some 2,826 square kilometers (almost 1,100 square miles)—outward from reactor No. 4. They would never be allowed to return.

> "The fruit orchards are heavy with unpicked, radioactive fruit that is left rotting on the branches."

Today, the exclusion zone remains almost entirely empty of human life. The fruit orchards are heavy with unpicked, radioactive fruit that is left rotting on the branches. Picket fences are slowly succumbing to entropy and collapsing. Vegetation is taking over the streets. The city of Prypiat—once a bustling Soviet city—is now an image of absolute decay, its wide boulevards empty but for the wind and the occasional wild boar or feral dog.

At one end of its once ostentatious main street, the city's cultural center still stands, debris spilling out of its front doors and down the stairs, wild rose bushes pushing through the cracks in the pre-fab, cement square outside. After the accident, it didn't take long for looters to discover Prypiat as a great source of furniture, windows and, in the case of the cultural center, stone tiles—tons of the radioactive bounty was carted away. When the disaster struck, the city was preparing for its annual May Day celebration. Hammer and sickle decorations installed two decades ago still hang from the lampposts; and behind the cultural center, an amusement

> "Living inside the zone is a macabre wager—that old age will do its damage before cancer takes hold.

park—Ferris wheel rusted, bumper cars overturned—is still waiting for children who will never come.

A Wager Against Cancer

Dangers still lurk within the exclusion zone. A short visit poses little health risk—it takes years for radiation to build up in the human body to a degree that will cause cancer, and radiation maps of the exclusion zone clearly highlight no-go areas. Visitors are equipped with an official government guide and a handheld Geiger counter; all food and water consumed in the zone is shipped in from the outside. Produce grown in the area's radioactive soil makes for an especially effective method of delivering radioactive isotopes directly into the bloodstream and bone marrow. But the dangers can't be seen. And other than the eerie desertion of the cities and villages in the exclusion zone, the disaster and contamination the Chernobyl disaster visited on the area remains completely invisible.

There are people who live within the exclusion zone. A number of older residents, unwilling to move away from the villages they lived in their entire lives, have returned. They receive food delivered from outside the zone along with regular medical checkups. For many, living inside the zone is a macabre wager—that old age will do its damage before cancer takes hold.

Today, the town of Chernobyl itself is likewise home to some 4,000 residents. Radiation from reactor No. 4 still leaks in dangerous amounts through substantial cracks in the makeshift cover installed in the months after the disaster. And scientists, geologists and workers are temporarily stationed in the less-irradiated buildings as they construct a new sarcophagus to safely cover the radioactive substances that remain. But the vast majority of those temporarily living in Chernobyl are forestry workers. Should the forests around Chernobyl catch fire, a new radioactive cloud would be set free.

Invisible Dangers

The town does have at least one permanent resident though. An Orthodox priest has taken charge of the Chernobyl church—a centuries old place of worship—to serve the souls who work there. It now sports a fresh coat of cheerful blue and white paint. As I walk through the doors on my visit, the priest is installing new heaters to keep his flock warm during the bitterly cold winter. It's easy to forget how risky the posting is, he says. "You can't see the dangers that lurk all around."

The drive back out of the exclusion zone follows the same empty highways we came in on. Back past the empty villages hidden in the dripping, snowy forest. Back to the guard hut. This time, two guards come out carrying radiation detectors. The car is swept; we are swept; the trunk is searched. Given a clean bill of health, we drive off into the gathering dusk toward Kiev, leaving the nuclear disaster zone behind us.

GLOSSARY

cesium-137   A radioactive isotope of cesium readily absorbed by the body and which has a half-life of 30.23 years.

curie   A measure of radioactivity equal to 37 billion radioactive atoms decaying per second; i.e., the amount of radioactivity released in one second by one gram of radium-226, a radioactive element discovered by Marie and Pierre Curie.

dosimeter   A device used to measure the absorbed dose of ionizing radiation.

exclusion zone   *see* Zone of Alienation.

gray   A measure of the "absorbed dose" of radiation, equal to the absorption of one joule of ionizing radiation by one kilogram of matter.

half-life   The amount of time expected for the radioactivity of a given sample to reduce by half. For example, iodine-131 has a half-life of approximately eight days. In a sample of eight iodine-131 atoms, four will decay over the course of the first eight days, two will decay over the next eight days, one will decay over the following eight days, and the entire sample will have likely decayed by the close of the next week.

iodine-131   A radioactive isotope of iodine having a half-life of just 8.0197 days, but which is easily absorbed by the thyroid gland (which requires iodine).

isotope   Different version of the same element. An element and its isotope have the same number of protons and electrons, but different numbers of neutrons (and thus different atomic masses); many isotopes have unstable nuclei, and are thus radioactive, releasing energy as their nuclei decay.

perestroika	An umbrella term for the economic and political reforms instituted in the Soviet Union by Mikhail Gorbachev in 1987.
potassium-40	A naturally occurring radioactive isotope of potassium; its exceptionally long half-life—1.25 billion years—makes it a significant environmental threat.
RBMK	Acronym for the Russian *reaktor bolshoy moshchnosti kanalniy*—literally, "high-power channel-type reactor," these reactors are characterized by having only partial containment structures (rather than full containment buildings, as with reactors built in the United States).
rem	Abbreviation for "roentgen equivalent man"; an outdated measure of the "equivalent dose" of radiation effectively absorbed by a person, replaced by the sievert, where 100 rem equal 1 sievert.
roentgen/röntgen	Unit for measuring ionizing radiation.
sievert	Measure of the "equivalent dose" of radiation, which attempts to take into account the different biological effects of different kinds of radiation on different tissues; equivalent dose is calculated by multiplying the absorbed dose (measured in gray) by several "quality factors" related to the type of radiation, type of tissue exposed, the time and volume over which the dosage was dispersed, and so on.
strontium-90	A potent radioactive isotope with a half-life of twenty-nine years. The body recognizes strontium-90 as calcium, readily absorbing it into bones and bone marrow, which can lead to bone cancer, leukemia, and cancers in adjacent tissues.
Zone of Alienation	(Also called the Prohibited Zone, Zone of Exclusion, Exclusion Zone, Chernobyl Zone, 30-kilometer Zone, and Fourth Zone) A 30 km (19 mile) zone surrounding the Chernobyl reactor established immediately following the disaster to mark the area of highest contamination; the zone straddles the Ukraine-Belarus border.

201

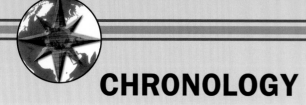
March 1984   Reactor four of the V.I. Lenin Nuclear Power Station near Chernobyl, Soviet Union, is brought online, despite concerns that the reactor may not be able to continue vital cooling operations during a power failure.

April 25, 1986   Morning: Dayshift workers prepare to run a test to confirm that the reactors' water-based cooling systems will function during power failure.

       2:00 P.M.: As part of the test, emergency core cooling systems are taken offline. Test postponed.

       11:04 P.M.: Experiment preparation resumes; experiment now to be run by unprepared nightshift workers.

April 26, 1986   1:23:04 A.M.: Experiment begins; temperatures in the reactor rapidly increases, as does power production.

       1:23:40 A.M.: The nightshift control rod operator initiates emergency shutdown, reinserting all of the graphite control rods; because of a flaw in the control rod design this causes a serious power spike.

       1:23:44 A.M.: The water-cooled reactor overheats, triggering a steam explosion that blows off the lid of the reactor core, damaging the building and exposing the reactor core to the open air; a second steam explosion ejects reactor fuel and burning graphite onto surrounding buildings.

1:28 A.M.: First firefighters arrive, many believing they have come to control an electrical fire.

8:00 A.M.: The plant's dayshift clocks in as usual.

April 27, 1986   Helicopters begin dropping sand, boron, and lead in an attempt to stop fires in reactor four; "temporary" evacuation of neighboring Pripyat begins.

Radiation is detected by the Forsmark Nuclear Power Plant in Sweden (700 miles away). Forsmark eventually attributes this to an as-of-yet unreported nuclear accident in the Soviet Union.

April 28, 1986   Soviet government announces that an accident has occurred.

May 2, 1986   Crews begin to tunnel beneath the damaged reactor in order to inject liquid nitrogen into the foundations, preventing the building's collapse and molten radioactive material from polluting the water table and causing another steam explosion.

May 6, 1986   Fire continues in reactor four, but emissions of radioactive isotopes drop by 98 percent for no known reason.

May 9, 1986   The first firefighter dies from acute radiation sickness

May 10, 1986   Fire in reactor four finally extinguished.

July 1986   Of the 237 rescue workers suffering acute radiation sickness, 28 have died by late July.

December 1986   Concrete "sarcophagus" completed, sealing off the reactor and its contents.

December 26, 1991   Soviet Union dissolves.

1997   Fund started to pay for "New Safe Confinement Structure" to contain the crumbling sarcophagus and its remaining 200 tons of radioactive debris.

2002   The "exclusion zone" surrounding reactor four is opened to tourists.

2004   Areas of Belarus contaminated with radioactive fallout from the explosion are opened to farming.

2012   New Safe Confinement Structure slated for completion; as of 2008, construction had yet to begin.

FOR FURTHER READING

Books

Glenn Alan Cheney, *Chernobyl: The Ongoing Story of the World's Deadliest Nuclear Disaster*. New York: New Discovery, 1993.

Michael J. Christensen and Michelle Carter, *Children of Chernobyl: Raising Hope from the Ashes*. Minneapolis: Augsburg, 1993.

Paul Fusco and Magdalena Caris, *Chernobyl Legacy*. Millbrook, NY: de.MO, 2001.

Robert Peter Gale and Thomas Hauser, *Final Warning: The Legacy of Chernobyl*. New York: Warner Books, 1989.

Arthur T. Hopkins, *Unchained Reactions*. Honolulu: University Press of the Pacific, 1994.

David R. Marples, *Chernobyl and Nuclear Power in the USSR*. New York: St. Martin's, 1986.

Trish Marx and Dorita Beh-Eger, *I Heal: The Children of Chernobyl in Cuba*. Minneapolis: Lerner, 1996.

Zhores A. Medvedev, *The Legacy of Chernobyl*. New York: Norton, 1992.

Richard Francis Mould, *Chernobyl Record*. London: Taylor & Francis, 2000.

Adriana Petryna, *Life Exposed: Biological Citizens After Chernobyl*. Princeton, NJ: Princeton University Press, 2002.

Piers Paul Read, *Ablaze: The Story of the Heroes and Victims of Chernobyl*. New York: Random House, 1993.

Iurii Shcherbak and David R. Marples, *Chernobyl: A Documentary Story*. New York: Palgrave Macmillan, 1989.

Alla Yaroshinska, *Chernobyl: The Forbidden Truth*. Lincoln: University of Nebraska Press, 1995.

Periodicals

Associated Press, "Chernobyl, Could It Happen Again?" MSNBC, April 24, 2006. www.msnbc.msn.com/id/12385593/.

C.J. Chivers, "New Sight in Chernobyl's Dead Zone: Tourists," *New York Times*, June 15, 2005.

Dixie Farley, Vern Modeland, and Dori Stehlin, "Chernobyl: 3 Years After," *FDA Consumer*, April 1989.

Henry Fountain, "Did Chernobyl Leave an Eden for Wildlife?" *New York Times*, August 28, 2007.

Angela Hill, "Bay Area Teen Now Thankful for Chernobyl Birth Defects," *Oakland (CA) Tribune*, May 1, 2006.

Ann Hornaday, "Straight Talk About Chernobyl," *Ms.*, August 1986.

Stephen Mulvey, Mark Kinver, and outside experts, "Q&A: Chernobyl 20 Years On," BBC, April 26, 2006. http://news.bbc.co.uk/l/hi/talking_point/4946456.stm.

François Murphy, "Chernobyl Radiation Death Toll 56 So Far—U.N." Reuters, September 5, 2005.

Steven Lee Myers, "First at Chernobyl, Burning Still," *New York Times*, April 26, 2006.

New York Times, "Chernobyl's Reduced Impact," September 8, 2005. www.nytimes.com/2005/09/08/opinion/08thu3.html?scp=16&sq=chernobyl&st=cse.

K.S. Parthasarathy, "Chernobyl's Legacy: Health Impacts," *Hindu*, September 15, 2005.

Richard Pérez-Peña, "In Throats of Émigrés, Doctors Find a Legacy of Chernobyl," *New York Times*, April 20, 2006.

Dana Priest, "Plant Is in Soviet Breadbasket," *Washington Post*, April 30, 1986.

Trey Ratcliff, "Nuclear Winter in Chernobyl," *Stuck in Customs*, February 2, 2007. www.stuckincustoms.com/2007/02/02/nuclear-winter-in-chernobyl/.

Boyce Rensberger, "Explosion, Graphite Fire Suspected." *Washington Post*, April 30, 1986.

Boyce Rensberger, "Partial Core Meltdown Suspected," *Washington Post*, April 29, 1986.

Elisabeth Rosenthal, "Experts Find Reduced Effects of Chernobyl," *New York Times*, September 6, 2005.

Geoff Smith, "Debate Still Rages over Chernobyl Fallout," *Financial Times*, November 18, 2008.

Wayne Snow, "Touring a Nuclear Ghost Town: Chernobyl," *Atlanta Journal-Constitution*, May 28, 2006.

Sunday Times (London), "Glad Tidings in the Shadow of Chernobyl," December 29, 2002. www.timesonline.co.uk/tol/news/article806301.ece.

Natalie Weinstein, "'Chernobyl Kid' Seeks Asylum from Anti-Semitism in Belarus," *J.*, September 6, 1996. www.jweekly.com/article/full/3975/chernobyl-kid-seeks-asylum-from-anti-semitism-in-belarus/

Carol J. Williams, "Soviet Media Offer Little Data on Accident; Kiev Effectively Put Off Limits," *Washington Post*, April 30, 1986.

Web Sites

The Chernobyl Children's Project International (www.chernobyl-international.com). The Chernobyl Children's Project International is a United Nations–recognized nongovernmental organization that brings aid to areas of Belarus and Ukraine affected by the Chernobyl disaster, especially focusing on the needs of children who have been orphaned in the wake of those regions' economic and social collapse. Since 1991, the organization has delivered $103 million in aid.

The Chernobyl Forum Website (www-ns.iaea.org). Organized under the auspices of the International Atomic Energy Agency, the Chernobyl forum includes nine United Nations agencies and the governments of Ukraine, Russia, and Belarus. The Chernobyl Forum was founded in 2003 to "scientifically clarify the radiological environmental and health consequences of the Chernobyl accident, to provide advice on and to contribute to a scientifically sound remediation and health care programmes."

Chernobyl.info (www.chernobyl.info). Maintained by the Swiss Agency for Development and Cooperation, Chernobyl. info is "the international communications platform on the long-term consequences of the Chernobyl disaster."

GreenFacts on the Chernobyl Nuclear Accident (www.green facts.org). GreenFacts is dedicated to aggregating scientific research and reports on environmental and health-related topics, then presenting this information in a manner accessible to nonspecialists and average citizens.

The United Nations and Chernobyl (http://chernobyl.undp .org). The official United Nations Web site dedicated to the Chernobyl disaster, its impact, and consequences.

Visit Sunny Chernobyl (www.visitsunnychernobyl.com). Visit Sunny Chernobyl is a Web log about "pollution tourism." It is run by Andrew Blackwell, a Canadian American writer and film editor.

INDEX

A

Abortions, 91
Acute radiation sickness, 6, 83–84, 129, 152, 159
Adamov, Yevgeny, 107, *110*
Advertising, 47–49
Agriculture, 59, 119–125
Aherne, Mary, 191
AIDS/HIV, 17, 80–81
Alamogordo (NM), 21
Alcoholism, 79, 160
Aleksandrov, A.P., 54–55
Alexievich, Svetlana, 172–183
Allergy problems, 75
Alpha radiation, 73
Anemia, 18
Animals
    contamination and, 8, 59, 115, 141, 180
    death toll from Chernobyl accident, 143
    genetic alteration and, *86*, 87
Antsipov, Gennadi V., 123–124
Armenia, 26, 31, 34, 57, 60
Artesian wells, 67
Associated Press, 128
Asthma, 143
Atlantic Ocean, 7, 25
Atomic bomb, 21–22, 24–25
Australia, 149
Austria, 7, 60
Azerbaijan, 26

B

Back to Chernobyl (TV program), 62
Background radiation, 72, 104, 149
Baltic Sea, 38
Barley, 120
BBC (British Broadcasting Company), 114, 154

Beaver, 8
Bees, 125
Belarus
    birth defects and, 92
    Chernobyl Children's Project International
        (CCPI), 101–102
    Chernobyl orphans and, 7
    Chernobyl-related deaths in, 97
    costs of Chernobyl accident, 96
    evacuation and resettlement of citizens, 67,
        104–105, 123
    exclusion zone, 94
    food product contamination, 98–99, 111
    Green Party, 97
    health issues in, 85, 105, 109–110, 160
    infant mortality rates, 109
    Institute of Radiation Security, 98
    international aid for, 94
    land contamination in, 93–99, 101–105,
        122–123
    minimization of Chernobyl accident impact
        and, 106–112
    nongovernment organization aid, 97
    as part of USSR, 26
    poverty in, 128–130
    psychological issues in, 121, 130
    radiation dispersal from Chernobyl accident
        and, 6, 14, 37, 93–99, 101–105, 122–123
    thyroid cancer in children and, 16, 18
    See also specific cities in Belarus
Belgium, 7
Beloyarsk station, 30, 49–50
Beria, Lavrentii, 23
Berries, 125
Beta radiation, 73, 83, 158
Bible, 174, 179
Birds, 8, 141, 152, 180
Birth defects
    cesium contamination and, 17
    "Chernobyl orphans" and, 7
    descriptions of, 81